Rescue

Also by Graeme Cook

Wings of Glory
None But the Valiant
Commandos in Action
Spotlight on Aircraft
Air Adventures
Break Out!
Sea Adventures
Weird and Wonderful Ships
Weird and Wonderful Aircraft
Sea Raiders
Survival Against All Odds
Amazing Vehicles at Work
Missions Most Secret
Silent Marauders
Small Boat Raiders
The Single-Handers

Rescue

Graeme Cook

HART-DAVIS, MACGIBBON
GRANADA PUBLISHING
London Toronto Sydney New York

Published by Granada Publishing in
Hart-Davis, MacGibbon Ltd 1978

Granada Publishing Limited
Frogmore, St Albans, Herts AL2 2NF
and
3 Upper James Street, London W1R 4BP
1221 Avenue of the Americas, New York, NY 10020 USA
117 York Street, Sydney, NSW 2000, Australia
100 Skyway Avenue, Toronto, Ontario, Canada M9W 3A6
Trio City, Coventry Street, Johannesburg 2001, South Africa
CML Centre, Queen & Wyndham, Auckland 1, New Zealand

ISBN 0 246 10947 5

Filmset in 'Monophoto' Baskerville 12 on 13 pt. and
printed in Great Britain by
Richard Clay (The Chaucer Press), Ltd,
Bungay, Suffolk

Contents

Acknowledgements

I should like to record my gratitude to those authors and publishers who granted me permission to draw upon their books and magazines for background and technical information. I am indebted also for the help given me by the staff of the Imperial War Museum, London; the Ministry of Defence (Army, Navy and Air); the United States Embassy, London; the Naval Attaché to the Federal German Embassy, London; the Curator and staff of the Royal Air Force Museum, Hendon; Miss V. Shrubsall of the Air Historical Branch, Ministry of Defence; the Curator of the Bundesarchiv, Koblenz, West Germany; and to the many private individuals who so generously gave of their time to recount personal wartime experiences and who made available documents which proved invaluable in my research. I owe a special debt to Fidelma for her constant encouragement and enthusiasm.

1

The Prisoners

At 04.45 hours on 1 September 1939, German air and land forces attacked Poland. The Second World War had begun. For the second time in thirty years Europe was plunged into conflict. It took the armed might of the Third Reich only eighteen days to crush Poland.

In the first five weeks of war, a British Expeditionary Force of 158,000 men and 25,000 vehicles, including tanks, was despatched to France. Britain's air force and navy stood posed for battle but for seven months there existed an uneasy peace. There were no great land or air battles. Although the 'phoney war', as that period came to be known, was not without incident, it was very largely a war of words with the adversaries growling at each other.

The British 'dug in', anticipating a German invasion of their shores and throughout the islands the population was on edge. The swift defeat of Poland had given them good cause for anxiety. Britain was ill-prepared for another war. Although she had a powerful navy, her army and air force were ill-equipped and unready.

On 3 September, the very day that Britain declared war on Germany, the British passenger ship *Athenia*, carrying among her passengers children bound for Canada, was torpedoed and sunk by a German U-boat off the coast of Ireland. On 17 September, the mighty aircraft carrier *Courageous* fell victim to another U-boat. But the most audacious attack of all came in October when the submarine U-47, under the command of Leutnant Gunther Prien, penetrated the stout defences of Britain's fleet base at Scapa Flow and sank the battleship *Royal Oak*, leaving Britain stunned.

It was the American press that coined the phrase 'phoney war' but there was nothing phoney about the war at sea. Merchant ship losses were devastating. In the first four months of war U-boats and surface raiders sank 114 vessels amounting to over 420,000 tons of shipping. Britain desperately needed a significant victory at sea to restore her confidence. And then it came, an epic encounter that was to raise the morale of the British and help fortify them in the face of the German menace. It culminated in a daring rescue which was to catch the imagination of the free world . . .

Germany could not hope to survive a confrontation with the British fleet on the surface and wisely avoided such an event at sea. Instead she hoped to strangle Britain into submission by whittling away at her merchant fleet using her U-boats and surface raiders.

In preparation for this war of attrition, the German High Command despatched surface warships out into the Atlantic. These were specially built armoured cruisers known as pocket battleships. They were light, fast and heavily armed. They were cunningly designed vessels that were too powerful to be sunk by destroyer or cruiser and too fast to be caught by the battleships of the British Navy which had the fire power to sink them. They could run amok in the Atlantic sinking Allied ships with impunity – or so the Germans thought.

One of these pocket battleships, the *Admiral Graf Spee*, under the command of Captain Langsdorf, left her base at Wilhelmshaven on 23 August 1939. With her 11-inch guns, a speed of 26 knots and a range of 12,500 miles, she was ideally suited for the task of surface raider, but Hitler's hand restrained her for a time. The Führer was anxious to sue for peace with Britain. He had already

shown what his forces could do and now he imagined
that Britain would submit. But when it became clear
that the British were determined to fight it out, he gave
way to the persuasion of Admiral Raeder, and the surface raiders were let loose upon the merchant ships.
The result was wholesale slaughter by *Graf Spee* in the
south Atlantic. In less than four months nine British
ships sank under her guns at points across the breadth
of the south Atlantic and into the Indian Ocean. Nothing, it seemed, could stop *Graf Spee* and the Royal Navy
despatched groups of warships to track her down and
destroy her. One of these groups was Force G, under
the command of Commodore Harwood, flying his flag
in the cruiser *Ajax*. With him were the cruisers *Exeter*
and *Achilles*.

Harwood's greatest problem was finding *Graf Spee* in
the vast expanse of the south Atlantic. Then at dawn on
13 December, Captain Langsdorf made a grave mistake
when he sighted the cruiser *Exeter*. Mistaking the British
ship for a convoy escort, he engaged her. It was too late
when he realised that she was not alone. At 06.17
hours, *Graf Spee* opened fire. Although out-numbered,
she could easily out-gun the British cruisers but they did
have superior manoeuvrability. The pocket battleship's
11-inch guns turned on *Exeter* and in less than twenty
minutes reduced her to a blazing hulk.

Now the German turned on *Achilles* and *Ajax*,
damaging them both. Then, unexpectedly, *Graf Spee*
belched smoke and headed north, apparently making
an escape bid. She had been hit several times by accur-
ate fire from the British warships but had sustained only
slight damage. In the exchange Langsdorf had been
wounded, a factor which is said to have caused his
subsequent errors of judgement.

Achilles and *Ajax* clung tenaciously to the German
ship, attempting torpedo attacks which failed. But they
got too close to the raider and she turned on them. *Ajax*
took the lion's share of the shelling and was severely

damaged. Then *Graf Spee* broke off the engagement and fled, still tailed by the damaged cruisers.

It was at this point that Langsdorf made an inspection of his ship and declared that she would have to put into port for repairs. She had been hit seventeen times but was far from unseaworthy. Nevertheless, Langsdorf put into the River Plate where he dropped anchor.

Achilles and *Ajax* stood sentinel over the mouth of the river, fully aware that neither of them could stop *Graf Spee* if she attempted to break out. Already the Admiralty was despatching a powerful force to come to their aid but it would take some five days before it could reach the River Plate. At all costs Langsdorf had to be persuaded to sit sight and, by a masterpiece of bluff and deception, he was convinced that the British force had already arrived and were waiting for him at the mouth of the river.

On the Sunday morning that followed, eight hundred men from *Graf Spee*'s crew were taken ashore, then she set sail in concert with a German merchant ship. But instead of breaking out into the Atlantic, she stopped again in shallow waters and off-loaded more of her crew. Onlookers on shore waited anxiously for Langsdorf's next move. They could not understand what he was up to, but then *Graf Spee* began to settle in the water. Shortly afterwards she burst into flames amid a series of violent explosions. Langsdorf was scuttling her. For four days she burned before finally fizzling out, a tangled wreck. (It is said she was later bought from Uruguay by the British Admiralty for £14,000.) Langsdorf committed suicide. But that was by no means the end of the story.

Throughout her time in the south Atlantic, *Graf Spee* had been attended by the supply ship *Altmark*. It was to this ship that Langsdorf transferred the prisoners he had taken from the British ships he had sunk. On 6 December, before the demise of the *Graf Spee*, the two ships met in mid-Atlantic and more prisoners were put

on board *Altmark* bringing the tally of prisoners to 299
Allied officers and men. Langsdorf, very much a sailor
of the old school, illustrated his concern for the welfare
of the prisoners by personally inspecting their quarters
on board *Altmark* and transferring carpets and other
fittings to the German ship from the British merchantman *Huntsman* before he sent her to the bottom. In
addition to this, some of the raider's spoils of tea and
cotton were transferred to the *Altmark* for transporation
to Germany.

When news of *Graf Spee*'s fate in the Plate estuary
reached Captain Dahl, the commander of the *Altmark*,
he set course north, bent upon breaching the British
blockade of the North Sea and delivering his prisoners
to the POW camps in Germany.

The German ship squirmed through the blockade by
taking the route between Iceland and the Faeroe
Islands, then she turned south. Dahl knew that he
would stand little chance of survival in the open North
Sea which was patrolled by British warships and aircraft. But there was an alternative, if illegal, course
open to him. That was to seek sanctuary in neutral
Norwegian waters and hug the coast of Norway where
British ships would, if they abided by the laws of
neutrality, be unable to harm her.

Dahl's plan depended upon the Norwegians not
discovering that his was a ship of war carrying
prisoners. If his ruse were discovered, Dahl would be
forced to release his prisoners into Norwegian custody.
In Berlin preparations were afoot to give Dahl a rous-
ing reception with his prize prisoners. The authorities
were anxious to wrest some kudos from the ignominious
fate of *Graf Spee*. Dahl, a former POW in the First
World War, saw his chance for glory and would stop at
nothing to reach Germany.

To pass the inevitable inspection by the Norwegian
coastal patrols, he stripped his vessel of its guns and
headed into Norwegian territorial waters, posing as an

innocent German oil tanker. She certainly had the appearance of a tanker. The prisoners were tightly confined in appalling conditions below decks with no ventilation or light. Dahl dared not let them be seen by the Norwegians. It was by then mid-February 1940. Norway was in the grip of winter and her rugged coastline was white with snow. Dahl felt secure.

On 14 February three RAF reconnaissance aircraft on patrol over the North Sea sighted a vessel they thought might be *Altmark*. Their uncertainty was due to the varying descriptions they had been given of the ship. The British, having discovered that the prisoners from *Graf Spee* had been transferred to the *Altmark*, were mounting a massive rescue operation to grab the prisoners before they reached Germany.

At that time a force of British warships, comprising the cruiser *Arethusa* and the destroyers *Cossack, Intrepid, Ivanhoe, Maori* and *Sikh*, was at large in the Skagerrak under the command of Captain Phillip Vian. They were abroad seeking out German iron ore ships crossing the Skagerrak from Norway to Germany. They were warned of *Altmark*'s suspected presence off the Norwegian coast and an Admiralty signal was handed to Vian. It read: '*Altmark* your objective. Act accordingly.' Vian turned north and the hunt was on.

In the meantime, however, *Altmark* had been inspected by the Norwegian coastal patrols and passed the test. Dahl had succeeded in convincing them that *Altmark* was nothing more than an innocent merchantman and two coastal patrol boats were escorting her south through territorial waters.

The hunt for *Altmark* was fraught with difficulties for Vian. The coastal waters of Norway were abuzz with all kinds of shipping, among which the German ship could be lost to the searchers. It was possible that *Altmark* could pass without being seen, since the snow white coast was punctuated by patches of dark, dry ground. This made pinpointing the ship against that background extremely difficult. To make matters worse, storm conditions prevailed in the North Sea.

On 16 February RAF aircraft claimed to have spotted her, but from each aircraft came conflicting positions. It was obvious to the flotilla commander that innocent ships were being mistaken for *Altmark* by the RAF pilots. He therefore decided to split his force so as to cover a wider area. He despatched *Arethusa*, *Intrepid* and *Ivanhoe* to search a northern area while he in *Cossack* scoured the south coast of Norway along with *Maori* and *Sikh*.

To say that the search was difficult would be an understatement. Vian did not know what the *Altmark* looked like. The only clue he had was a photograph of two ships in the London *Evening News*. The picture showed two merchantmen close by each other at sea, one a four-masted ship in the foreground and the other a two-masted vessel. The caption did not indicate which of them was the *Altmark*. (In fact the four-master was the merchantman *Huntsman* from which Dahl had helped himself to booty.) Vian opted for the four-master, since the other had the appearance of being a tanker.

To add to Vian's growing frustration, he caught sight of a 'German' ship and chased her, only to discover that she was an innocent Swedish craft.

But the day was saved when a young officer on board the *Arethusa* sighted a ship in the far distance hugging the coast with what looked like an escort of Norwegian gun boats. *Arethusa* changed course to close in on the craft and as she drew nearer the German ensign became visible together with the incriminating name *Altmark* painted in white letters on the ship's stern. They had found her but now came the most difficult action of all.

According to the laws of neutrality, British warships had no right to enter Norwegian waters and intercept any ship, no matter what her nationality. But the

Admiralty had decided that the risk of offending Norway had to be taken and *Arethusa*'s captain ordered his destroyers in to intercept and board *Altmark*. But the Norwegian navy was having none of it. The two patrol boats escorting *Altmark* slipped one on either side of her, preventing the British destroyers from getting a boarding party on her. *Arethusa*'s captain dared not fire upon the Norwegians since the repercussions of such a violent act against an innocent neutral would be enormous. But then of course there were the prisoners battened down under the hatches, suffocating in the stench-filled holds.

It was not long before the action was decided for them. *Altmark* put on a burst of speed and slid into Josing Fjord, a narrow canyon of water about a mile long with a neck no wider than two hundred yards. The fjord was partially frozen over and *Altmark*'s bows cut through the ice as she surged forward, while the two patrol boats, both of which carried torpedoes, took up station at the mouth of the fjord.

It was at this point that Vian arrived on the scene in *Cossack*. After the frustrations of the previous forty-eight hours Vian was in no mood for interference from the Norwegian boats. Positive action was required and he was just the man to take it. He ferreted out an RNVR officer who spoke both Swedish and German and told him to ask the captain of the motor torpedo boat *Kjell* to come on board *Cossack* so that they might discuss the situation. The captain obliged but Vian soon found that he would get no co-operation from him. He told Vian that *Altmark* had already been searched three times since she entered Norwegian waters and no prisoners had been found. Clearly this was either a blatant lie or the searchers had done a very poor job. It would take a blind man to miss 299 men on board what was, after all, a comparatively small ship. Vian's anger was growing and he had to restrain himself from losing his temper. But the Norwegian captain had not finished.

He told Vian that he was under orders to fire upon the British ships if they should make any attempt to board *Altmark* and he pointed out that the torpedo tubes of his patrol boats were pointing directly at *Cossack*. They had reached an *impasse*. Any belligerent move made by Vian now could prove embarrassing and costly. He wisely decided to signal the Admiralty for instructions.

At that time in the war, Winston Churchill was First Lord of the Admiralty and it occurred to Vian that Churchill himself had had a hand in the reply he received. It spelled out in clear and precise language Vian was to do:

> Unless Norwegian torpedo boat undertakes to convoy *Altmark* to Bergen with a joint Anglo-Norwegian guard on board and a joint escort, you should board *Altmark*, liberate the prisoners and take possession of the ship pending further instructions. If Norwegian torpedo boat interferes, you should warn her to stand off. If she fires upon you, you should not reply unless attack is serious, in which case you should defend yourself using no more force than is necessary and cease fire when she desists. Suggest to Norwegian that honour is served by submitting to superior force.

Vian's course was now clear and he closed in on the Norwegians and asked them once more to stand aside. But the Norwegian captain remained stubborn. By now Vian was seriously worried that the Germans might be planning an air attack on his ships, and the longer he stayed the greater the hazard.

Vian manoeuvred *Cossack* into a position where he could bring his guns to bear upon the Norwegians and where their torpedoes would miss the ship if they fired. He then warned the Norwegian commander that he would open fire if he did not get out of the way. Seeing that the result would be annihilation, the Norwegian ordered his boats out of the way.

Cossack's engines throbbed as she put on speed and slipped into the mouth of the fjord. The guns' crews stood to, ready for the word to open fire if there was resistance from *Altmark*. Vian was unaware that Dahl had stripped *Altmark* of her guns for the passage through Norwegian waters. Speed and surprise were of the essence and *Cossack* lanced up the channel of ice-bound water, her bows carving a path through the ice until finally she rounded a bend and found her target.

A boarding party under Lieutenant Turner was ready to make the leap on to the prison ship. Turner was to go first, followed immediately by Petty Officer Atkins. They were to fasten a line across which the remainder of the boarding party would scramble to the *Altmark*.

The German ship was stuck fast in the ice with her bows to the shore but when she sighted *Cossack* her engines throbbed and her screw thrashed the water at her stern in a bid to reverse out of her position. Her intention became clear. She was bent upon ramming the destroyer and only by *Cossack*'s deft handling was this avoided. Dahl switched on his ship's searchlight and played it on to *Cossack*'s bridge hoping to blind Vian as he manocuvred his ship towards the other.

Evasive action had to be taken quickly; Dahl's plan was thwarted and *Cossack* slid alongside the stern of *Altmark*.

Turner timed his jump with perfection, landing with a thud on *Altmark*'s deck. Atkins thrust himself into the air, missed the *Altmark*'s deck and only just managed to grab the rim of the ship's side. For a moment he hung desperately there, clinging on for dear life. If he were to fall he would be crushed between destroyer and prison ship. But Turner grabbed him and hauled him on board. In a few moments they had a line attached and the others of the boarding party were making their way over it.

The boarding party, armed with a variety of

weapons, including knives and rifles, swarmed over the ship. Turner launched himself towards the bridge, scaling the ladder three rungs at a time. Both ships were still moving. He reached the bridge and waved his gun in Dahl's face, threatening to shoot if he did not surrender immediately. Dahl, no hero now, sensing that all was lost, gave in, as did the other officers on the bridge, except one, who clearly sought a glorious – and early – path to the grave. He grabbed the ship's telegraph and changed it. Turner cocked his revolver and levelled it at the man. The officer backed off and raised his arms in submission.

The two ships were held together by the boarding party's line and their combined manoeuvres were forcing them stern-first into the shore. Vian saw that *Cossack* might be grounded. He cut the connecting line and drew clear while *Altmark* rammed the shore.

On board *Altmark* were several armed guards from *Graf Spee*, put there to keep an eye on the prisoners. They felt duty bound to put up a fight, and before news of Dahl's surrender had reached them one of them shot Gunner Smith of the boarding party. The sound of the shot heralded the opening of a running battle with the guards. They soon realised that they were getting the worst of the exchange and they leapt off the ship and scurried into the shore and up the steep incline. Then they took up positions overlooking *Altmark* and opened fire. Turner and his men replied. The Germans were easy targets thrown into relief against the white snow and they fell rapidly.

Below decks the prisoners could hear the battle raging above them, but they had no idea what was happening. At last silence fell. Six Germans were dead and another six seriously wounded. Only the unfortunate Gunner Smith had sustained injury on the British side and his wound was not serious.

With the Germans subdued, Turner and his men set about hacking at the hatches until they broke through.

They peered down into the inky darkness and one of them yelled, 'Any British down there?'

Out of the hold came a concerted shout. 'Yes, we're all British!'

'Come on up, then!' Turner bawled. 'The Navy's here!'

It was over and the prisoners were freed. 299 men who had given up hope of seeing their families again had been rescued at the eleventh hour, thanks to the courage and daring of Vian and the crew of *Cossack*.

The survivors of the *Altmark*'s crew were taken on board *Cossack* along with the British prisoners and shipped back to Britain where Dahl, who had been poised for triumph, was put into a POW camp for the second time.

News of Vian's daring rescue, coupled with the demise of the *Graf Spee*, had the desired effect. It proved to be the vital morale booster that raised the hopes of the British nation – but it was to have serious consequences for the Norwegians.

Historians have claimed that the unwillingness of the Norwegian gun boats to do battle with the British warships was a clear sign that Norway was a willing ally of Britain. There were even suggestions by the Norwegian pro-Nazi Vidkun Quisling, that the whole thing was a put-up job. Adolf Hitler had been undecided about invading Norway but it is said that these suppositions did much to sway him in favour of invasion and this he did with terrible consequences.

Hitler's invasion of Norway and the resulting clash between the German and Allied forces there was to provide the scene for another epic and daring event in British naval history when a tiny craft pitted itself against the German Luftwaffe . . .

Hitler believed the Allies intended landing in Norway and using the country as a base from which to launch attacks against Germany's ill-defended Baltic ports and from these to strike at Berlin itself. This was no idle rumour. Plans were well advanced to make such a move. But Hitler was one step ahead of the Allies and he had already prepared an expeditionary force which was to invade Norway with the same speed as he had taken Poland. The Norwegian airfields would be a valuable asset to him in countering the British naval superiority in the North Sea. Norway's fjords would be perfect anchorages for Hitler's capital ships and from there they could venture out into the Atlantic. Norway therefore assumed considerable strategic importance both to Germany and the Allies.

The Allies were ready to land in Norway but inter-Allied squabbles about how this was to be done resulted in a stay of execution of three days. The delay was fatal, for it allowed Hitler's forces to thrust north into Norway and gain a foothold before the Allies could land.

The German invasion was swift and effective. It began on the morning of 9 April 1940 and German warships occupied the major ports from Oslo in the south round the coast as far north as Narvik within the Arctic Circle.

On land they fought their way north, capturing airfields to which Luftwaffe aircraft were despatched to give support to the ground and naval forces. With the airfields in German hands, the battle was all but over. As in many battles that were to follow, it was he who controlled the sky who won the day.

Britain and France marshalled their forces to repel the invading Germans. Between 15 and 16 April the Allies landed from the sea at three points to face severe opposition from the Germans. One of their landing points was at the port of Namsos. Lacking in experience and ill-equipped for such a task, the Allied invasion's fate was almost a foregone conclusion, particularly since the Luftwaffe reigned supreme in the skies.

Like all the ports on the Norwegian west coast,

Namsos lies deep inland at the end of a narrow fjord, protected from the rigours of the North Sea. Until the arrival of foreign forces, Namsos had been the central port from which timber in the area was exported. There were three quays available for loading the timber; one a large stone quay from which ocean-going ships could take on cargo; the second a smaller wooden quay at Namsos itself, and a third, a similar one, not far off. It was to those quays that the Allied force headed on 16 and 17 April. Despite intense aerial bombardment from the Luftwaffe, troops were landed and they moved inland to wage war upon the Germans. But the quality of the German troops was exceedingly high and the Allies were without sufficient artillery and lacked experience. They fought with courage but that was not enough. The battle was not going their way and they retreated towards Namsos for re-embarkation. It was when they reached the shambles of Namsos which had been flattened by Luftwaffe bombing that the slaughter began in earnest. Everything that moved was subjected to almost continuous bombing from Stuka dive bombers, most notably the ships in the fjord which had no room to manoeuvre out of harm's way.

Among these craft was a group of anti-submarine trawlers. The intention was that they should patrol the entrance to the fjord and search for German submarines heading into the fjord. However, their Asdic submarine detection equipment was ineffective in the narrow waters of the fjord. Worse still, they had little or no defensive armament with which to fight off air attack. Most were equipped with Lewis guns and some with an additional Oerlikon 20-millimetre gun. To add to their vulnerability they were slow and difficult to manoeuvre. They took a terrible pounding. After several of them had been hit and either sunk or totally disabled, the survivors were forced to take cover inshore under over-hanging cliffs, throughout the daylight hours. Of a force of twenty-nine trawlers sent to the area, eleven were sunk or disabled. The fact that any of them survived at all was due very largely to the skill and determination of their crews. They were manned mainly by former fishermen and commanded by officers of the Royal Naval Reserve who came from the Merchant Navy or were former trawler skippers.

The trawlers operated in groups of four and one group came under the overall command of Commander Sir Geoffrey Congreve, a retired Royal Navy officer. The 15th Anti-Submarine Striking Force, as the small four-boat group was known, comprised the trawlers *Arab, Aston Villa, Angle* and *Gaul*. Of these, one was to gain particular distinction. She was *Arab*, under the command of Lieutenant Commander Richard Been Stannard.

The 15th ASSF arrived off Namsos on the morning of 28 April along with another similar force and made their way down the fjord to Namsos. Immediately they arrived, Stannard and *Arab* were given a job to do. The cruiser *Carlisle* lay off Namsos and was loaded with stores, ammunition and equipment for the French troops on shore. Stannard's job was to ferry these goods to the shore. The work had not progressed very far when the first light of dawn lit the fjord and brought with it a flight of German dive-bombers.

Carlisle was among their targets and since *Arab* was at that time alongside, Stannard cast off to give the cruiser a chance to manoeuvre out of the way. The bombs erupted in the freezing fjord casting mountainous columns of icy water into the air.

The attack did not last long and calm returned to the fjord, Stannard took *Arab* alongside the cruiser and returned to the chore of off-loading the stores. But the Luftwaffe was certain to return and they did, this time in even greater strength.

When the Stukas struck again *Arab* was tied up at the quay behind a French transport ship, the *Saumur*, which had arrived the previous day laden with ammunition.

The wail of the dive-bombers prompted her French master to slip away from the pier which was a natural target for the bombers. But in the panic to flee a wire wrapped itself round the transport's screw and she drifted helplessly a little way out in the fjord. Meanwhile Stannard was busy off-loading the ammunition and he was not to be interrupted, air raid or no. He leapt ashore and rounded up some French and British soldiers whom he put to work unloading the ammunition. They had stacked the boxes on the quay when the attention of the Stukas was drawn to the pier and they closed in for the kill. One bomb would be enough to do it. A Stuka flung itself vertically down and released its bomb which hit the pile of ammunition and exploded, blasting it to kingdom come and setting fire to the wooden quay. Luckily *Arab* was well below the line of the quay and the explosion swept right across her, causing only slight damage. A blazing inferno leapt out from the quay and threatened to set the *Saumur* on fire with her load of ammunition. There seemed to be nothing she could do to escape the flames.

Stannard saw her predicament and *Arab* and her sister ship *Angle* went to her rescue. *Angle* was the first there; she got a line across and pulled *Saumur* clear of the flames. It was then that Stannard saw that they would lose the valuable pier if the fire was not put out. Without the pier, re-embarkation of the troops would be made much more difficult. Throwing caution to the wind he took *Arab* in and nosed her bows against the wooden structure with engines running slowly to keep the trawler in position. Then he got the hoses working and he and the others took turns at playing water on the fire for the next two hours while bombs fell around them. Stannard succeeded in saving the little quay before having to withdraw. When the evacuation later came, the little bit of pier Stannard had saved was of immense value to the ships and boats taking off the troops.

The Luftwaffe kept up its bombardment throughout the morning and into the afternoon. *Angle* had to leave the *Saumur* and *Arab* took her place until eventually the wire which was fouling her propeller was freed. The two vessels locked together were ideal targets, and bombs churned up the water around them but neither vessel was struck.

The stalwart crew of *Arab* was exhausted. They had had no sleep for forty-eight hours but under Stannard's persuasive leadership they battled on without complaint. Their work was far from done. It was learned that the mass evacuation of troops was to take place throughout the nights of 1 and 2 May. *Arab* and *Angle* were called to help. There was a French battalion of some 850 men ready to be re-embarked on to two transports in the fjord, and throughout the night the two trawlers ferried men out to the waiting ships until at last all the Frenchmen were on board the transports.

But there was to be no respite for the trawlers' crews. Dawn had no sooner arrived than the German bombers appeared. Stannard had now to seek shelter. *Arab* was just one of the bombers' targets and in less than an hour she suffered sixteen near misses. The concussion of the explosions damaged her rudder and propeller and cracked castings in the engine room. Luckily she remained afloat. Stannard dodged the falling missiles as best he could and made his way up the fjord towards the mouth, where Congreve was stationed in the trawler *Aston Villa*.

Throughout that morning, *Arab* was harassed by marauding bombers which kept up an aerial onslaught upon the ships in the fjord, concentrating upon the trawlers which were soon the only vessels left there. Stannard's skill in dodging the bombs saved *Arab* but the Commander's trawler was not so lucky. Near misses transformed her into a floating wreck and she was so badly mauled that she could barely move.

Congreve told Stannard to find shelter away from

the menace of the Stukas and *Arab* sought succour under an over-hanging cliff. She was safe – at least for the moment. But the *Gaul* failed to reach sanctuary. A bomb hit her in the bows, tearing a fifteen-foot hole in her. Severely crippled, she limped into a narrow inlet to hide out. As a fighting ship she was finished. She could barely remain afloat. The trawler strength was being relentlessly whittled down.

But there came a small ray of hope in the arrival of the sloop *Bittern*. From the point of view of the trawlers, she might prove their saviour since the German pilots would concentrate upon the large ship when they resumed their bombing the following day. Stannard, his anger aroused, was determined to swat some of these flies from the sky and he devised a plan to do just that. When darkness overtook the fjord, he took *Arab* alongside *Bittern* and had a conference with the sloop's captain.

Stannard had noticed that the German aircraft always attacked out of the sun, blinding the British gunners and he saw a way of using this to his advantage. He would position *Arab* about 400 yards to the west of *Bittern* so that when the bombers had plunged down and were rearing skyward out of their dive, their bellies would be exposed to his gunners. The captain agreed and when, the next day, sixteen dive-bombers screeched down upon *Bittern* then pulled up, they met the full force of Stannard's guns which raked them with machinegun and Oerlikon fire. The gunners scored hit after hit and many of the Stukas limped off badly wounded, some so severely damaged that they crash-landed before they could reach their bases.

Stannard's turkey shoot had to be brought to an end when Congreve called him away. The Commander had to find out the extent of the damage to *Gaul* and Stannard was to take him for an inspection. They set off and en route found what remained of the *St Goran* which had been part of the other trawler force. She was

in a pitiful state, hugging the shore beneath the over-
hang of a tree-clad cliff. When they got close they found
one of her lifeboats containing seriously wounded men
together with rafts on which other members of the crew
lay. A bomb had scored a direct hit on *St Goran*'s
bridge, killing the captain and three others.

Bombs were falling around *Arab* and the disabled
trawler as Stannard rescued the crew from the boat and
the rafts. Despite their own exhaustion, *Arab*'s crew set
to doing what they could for the wounded while
Stannard took the trawler into the protection of the
shore. Fortunately help arrived not long after, when the
destroyer *Janus* hove into sight. Stannard signalled her
and she sent over her surgeon and a sick berth attendant. Then she sped off towards Namsos.

The situation of the trawlers was desperate and
Stannard lost no time in signalling Admiral Vivian to
that effect. But sympathetic as the Admiral was to their
plight, he insisted they hold their ground. He had
heard that both U-boats and enemy surface warships
were on their way and every gun would be needed.
Stannard sighed and bent himself to the task. The
chances of getting out of the fjord alive were remote
indeed. But he would fight with every ounce of his
strength and resource to rescue his crew and their
vessel.

There was no let-up in the bombing which had been
diverted to the major warships near Namsos. *Bittern* was
hit. Her stern was blown off and she sank. But *Carlisle*
came forging down the fjord and paused to take on the
wounded whom Stannard and his crew had been tend-
ing. Relieved of his charges and still determined to
subtract a few more aircraft from the Luftwaffe,
Stannard considered how he could best put up a
defence against air attack on *Arab* and *Gaul* which
was lying beside her. He decided to mount machineguns on the cliff top where they would have a clear
field of fire into the air, down upon enemy ships or

inland against ground forces. On board *Arab* he found a mortar with ammunition and rifles which had been left by the French. Throughout the day, he and his crew worked to set up their redoubt on the cliff top. By the evening he had six Lewis guns, two rifles and the mortar in position together with the *Arab*'s own fixed weapons.

Stannard made another useful find in the shape of a cave in the cliff side. There his crew was able to take turns in sleeping throughout the night that followed.

Dawn came and they searched the sky for the dive-bombers. As they were doing so, *Aston Villa* crept inshore and tied up about a hundred yards from *Arab*. Shortly afterwards, the Stukas arrived and focused their attention upon the three trawlers. The bombing was kept up throughout the morning and it was *Gaul* that got the worst of it. Near misses split her wide open and at 13.30 hours she sank. But Stannard's defenders had put up a heroic fight, lashing the diving aircraft with fire. Stubborn as their resistance was, however, there was no doubt that it would not be long before the other two boats met a similar fate. Stannard wisely decided to bring as many of the crews ashore as could be spared and left only the guns' crews on the two trawlers.

During the afternoon the inevitable happened. A bomb struck *Aston Villa* and she was set on fire, injuring four men. They were rescued and brought up the cliff on improvised stretchers.

For the remainder of the day *Aston Villa* blazed fiercely and she threatened to blow up. If that happened, *Arab* would undoubtedly be taken with her. Around 20.00 hours Stannard cut *Arab* loose from her moorings and with two other men hauled her along the shore using thick ropes. They had not gone far when *Aston Villa* exploded – but he had saved *Arab*.

At Namsos the evacuation of the troops was in full swing and Stannard took *Arab* there to put the wounded and the crews of the other trawlers on board the evacuation ships. With this completed, he was ordered to strike out for the open sea and he set course for the mouth of the fjord. It was a long and perilous journey, crawling at a mere three knots but *Arab* struggled along until, by dawn, she was clearing the mouth of the fjord. But Stannard's fight to save his ship was by no means over. He knew that, moving as slowly as he was, *Arab* would be easy prey for enemy aircraft and his fears were realised when a lone Heinkel 115 flew overhead and signalled him to turn east or be sunk. Stannard gave him a metaphorical 'two fingers' and when the aircraft came within range firing machinegun bullets at the trawler, Stannard replied with every gun he had. The enemy aircraft went down like a stone, riddled with bullets.

Arab eventually reached Britain and safety. Stannard had courageously rescued his trawler and her crew from what seemed to be certain death. For his courage he was awarded the Victoria Cross, the second to be awarded to a naval officer in the Second World War.

2

Jungle Marauders

'If ever there was a hell on earth, it was Burma.'

There could have been few who fought in that country in the Second World War who did not share that sentiment. Disease, impenetrable jungle and a suicidally determined enemy combined to make that theatre of war unsurpassed for misery and privation. Add to that lethal animals and insects crowding the undergrowth, together with clammy, soaking heat, inadequate rations, insufficient water and lack of proper medical supplies and you have a cameo of the Burma battleground. And yet, against all these odds, Allied soldiers did battle with the most disciplined armed forces in the world – the Imperial Japanese Army – and won.

When thinking of the war in Burma the lay person might be forgiven for imagining that it was the exclusive preserve of the British and Commonwealth armies. But it was not so. There were other ground forces who played an important part in routing the Japanese in Burma, among them the United States Army. One naturally thinks of the US Army storming ashore on countless beaches in the Pacific on its island-hopping campaign. But the US Army fought with equal valour – if not equal numbers – in South-East Asia.

The 5307th Composite Unit (Provisional), United States Army, to give it its official title, ranks among the most famous US Army forces to fight in the war and it won its spurs in the jungles of Burma . . .

It took the Japanese only four months to drive the Allies 900 miles out of Burma in 1942. The Jap soldier was a fanatical fighter. Little wonder that after his 'lightning' victory he was seen as superhuman, invincible in battle, unconquerable in the jungle. But the truth was that the Japanese soldier was no more invincible than his Occidental opponent; he bled just as surely from his wounds; he was no marksman and no more at home in the jungle than a Briton, American or Australian. The Japanese won the battle for Burma because they controlled the air and the sea and the Allies lacked artillery, transport and reinforcements. The outcome was inevitable.

The Allied retreat and subsequent defeat caused a serious fall in morale and it was clear that if they were to oust the enemy from Burma, a spirit of optimism had to be instilled in the battle-weary army that had been driven across the border into India. A victory was needed to shatter for ever the image of Japanese invincibility. It was to come in a dramatic and unconventional way.

Among those thrust out of Burma in 1942 was an American lieutenant-general who commanded a Chinese army which had crossed the border into Burma to help stem the tide of advancing Japanese. He was Joseph Stilwell, a sixty-year-old veteran of the First World War. Stilwell was known throughout the army as 'Vinegar Joe' – and not without reason. A courageous and dedicated soldier, he had a venomous side to his nature. As commander of the Chinese army in Burma he was responsible to Generalissimo Chiang Kai-shek, whom he nicknamed 'the peanut'. He described his chief as 'a grasping, bigoted, ungrateful little rattlesnake', at the head of a government comprised of 'a gang of thugs'. He had another serious bias; Stilwell was an anglophobe who made no secret of his dislike for the British. He viewed them contemptuously and insisted that they 'were not interested in the war in the

Pacific'. When referring to them he invariably used the term 'Goddam Limeys', a turn of phrase hardly likely to endear him to his allies. However, prejudice was by no means unique to Stilwell; there were other commanders among the Allies who had equally deep-rooted biases.

Stilwell felt the humiliation of defeat strongly and itched to smash the Japanese, using his Chinese army. He had his own pet theories as to how this could be done. Unfortunately for Allied harmony, his ideas differed from those of the British. Stilwell opposed the British idea that the recapture of Burma was of key importance. He was heavily, perhaps understandably, in favour of a Chinese initiative. This meant that his priority lay in opening a route from India, the main supply dump, through north Burma to China. With such a supply route open he could transport and supply a Chinese army which he would build and train in India then move along the Burma road to China to do battle with the Japanese. At that time China was supplied by air from India over the 17,000-foot-high Himalayas, the route known as the 'Hump'.

Stilwell fervently believed that a road to China could be built from the railhead at Ledo in Assam. Using the Chinese troops he would train at a base in India, he would push the Japs back into south Burma and allow his engineers and native labour to build the road behind his lines. It was an ambitious project and Stilwell got support for it back home in the US where it mattered. But the British were opposed to it. Prime Minister Churchill was against the scheme, so was General Slim, commander of the British 14th Army in India. He later said of Stilwell's plan:

The American amphibious strategy in the Pacific, of hopping from island to island would bring much quicker results than an overland advance across Asia with a Chinese army not yet formed. In any case, if the road was to be really effective, its feeder railway should start at Rangoon, not Calcutta. If it had been left to me, on military grounds, I would have used the immense resources required for this road, not to build a highway to China but to bring forward the largest possible combat forces to destroy the Japanese army in Burma. Once that was accomplished, the old route to China would be open; over it would flow a much greater tonnage than could ever come via Ledo.

The British opposition to Stilwell's plan reinforced his idea that the British were more interested in the war in Europe than in South-East Asia.

Stilwell had another opponent, this time within the US forces. He was General Claire Chennault, commander of the 14th US Air Force in China. Chennault maintained that he could rout the Japs from China with his air force, using the 152 aircraft available to him. President Roosevelt and Generalissimo Chiang Kai-shek agreed, with the result that the airborne supply route across the Hump was not used to ferry supplies to the Chinese army but principally to supply the air force.

The then C-in-C of the British forces in India, General Wavell, launched a small-scale offensive against the Japanese in the Arakan with the idea of achieving a swift victory and boosting the morale of the British and Indian troops as well as securing a base at Akyab for the future reconquest of Burma. The operation was a disaster and the raiders were pushed back over the border into Assam.

But a faint glimmer of hope lit the gloom. Earlier that year, in February 1942, Wavell had acquired an officer who was destined to have a striking effect upon the war in Burma. He was Orde Wingate, an advocate of unconventional warfare. He quickly saw the potential of small-scale strike forces in Burma and urged

Wavell to allow him to set up what he called 'Long-Range Penetration Groups'. His idea was that these groups would be trained in India to fight in the Burmese jungle and strike at the Japanese communications as well as their outposts, thus disrupting them and softening them up for the major reconquest. They would become experts in the art of jungle fighting, communications and the techniques of destruction. They would operate deep behind the enemy lines and to do so they would require their own, unique set-up. Wingate knew that ground and air co-operation would be crucial and he proposed that they should be supplied by regular air drops. To help them transport their equipment over the rough terrain they would take mules with them. The proposal appealed to Wavell and he gave it the green light. A small RAF unit was attached to the force to use its expertise in the selection of suitable dropping zones.

The poor morale of the Allied troops in India after their reversals in Burma urged Wingate to mount an early operation. Wingate's 'Chindits', as he called them, crossed the Chindwin River on the night of 14 February 1943. They split into two groups and began a series of devastating attacks on railway lines, bridges and Jap outposts. They ambushed enemy patrols and caused havoc wherever they went. The Chindits' losses were heavy and it must be said that Japanese casualties were slight but because of the attacks the Japs were obliged to move a large part of two divisions to counter the Chindits. In the bitter fighting the Chindits were forced to withdraw, leaving behind most of their equipment. But the Chindit incursion brought about a change in Japanese thinking and strategy which eventually led to their downfall. More than that, it destroyed for ever the myth that the Japs were masters of the jungle. The Allies could fight on equal terms.

While these operations were taking place, things were moving at a fast pace well away from the battlefront. At conferences in Washington, Casablanca and Quebec, the decision was taken to recapture north Burma and establish a land route to China.

At the Quebec Conference, Wingate was called to give his views on Long-Range Penetration Groups. He did it with vigour and conviction, so much so that he got the support of the American Chiefs of Staff. He advocated setting up jungle bases behind the enemy lines from which these groups could operate, causing confusion among the enemy as well as pin-pointing targets for the air force bombers. So impressed were the Americans with Wingate's ideas that they decided to call for volunteers for their own Long-Range Penetration Group, code-named 'Galahad'. They also resolved to set up a special air force group, Number One Air Commando, which would give air support to both their own and Wingate's groups. When Stilwell heard of the decision he was overwhelmed with delight. He had further cause to be in good humour. The arrangement of command of the forces in South-East Asia was changed when Admiral Lord Louis Mountbatten was appointed Supreme Allied Commander. Stilwell got on well with the new commander and sensed immediately that here was a man of drive and initiative. A new feeling of unity and co-operation was born.

Much had to be done before the major offensive to re-take the north of Burma could get underway. It had to be planned in infinite detail. Stilwell's Chinese divisions had to be trained in India before launching themselves into Burma using new weapons supplied by the Allies. And the formation and training of the American Long-Range Penetration Group had to be completed.

Stilwell's area of responsibility was a part of Upper Burma which included the Chindwin River and the Japanese-held airfield at Myitkyina. Japanese fighters were based there and they posed a considerable threat to the aircraft ferrying supplies over the Hump. So much so that the planes had to take a more northerly route. This meant carrying more fuel and less supplies. If Stilwell could take Myitkyina, it would mean securing a more direct route to China for Chennault's aircraft. There was yet another objective in thrusting into that area. If Stilwell could take the Hukawng and Mogaung valleys it would clear a path for his engineers building the road from Ledo and mean that they could link up with an existing road to China.

Stilwell moved his Chinese 22nd and 38th Divisions from their base in India to Ledo. Behind them would follow the road builders, carving a path in their wake. They began the push into Burma and almost immediately met stiff opposition. But it is with the American Long-Range Penetration Group that we are primarily concerned, a fighting force which was to be moulded into some of the toughest fighters in Burma.

The call for 'volunteers from experienced jungle troops for a dangerous mission' met with a quick response. Men came forward in their thousands but the will to fight was not enough. They had to be superbly fit and had to comply with myriad other prerequisites. The unsuitable were quickly weeded out and the force, about 3000 strong, assembled and shipped to India to undergo a gruelling and intensive training in jungle fighting. Wingate had done much to set the pattern of jungle training and it was on the experience of the Chindits that the training was based. The men were mercilessly driven to their physical limits. The food they were served was British and by American standards it was close to a starvation diet. But the Americans were nothing if not improvisers. The trainees found nice plump birds remarkably like turkeys which they shot and ate, unaware that they were devouring vultures.

The new force, designated the 5307th Composite Unit (Provisional), US Army, was divided into three battalions under the overall command of Brigadier-General Frank Merrill. The composition of the individual battalions was the same. Each one was commanded by a lieutenant-colonel. His battalion was split into two combat teams identified by colours. Within each of these combat teams were sixteen officers and 456 men. These were divided into a rifle company of three rifle platoons and a heavy weapon section, a heavy weapon platoon, a pioneer and demolition platoon, an intelligence and reconnaissance platoon and a medical detachment. This was the composition of the force but there was an addition which was to prove invaluable, as Wingate had found. The whole regiment had at its disposal some 700 mules to carry packs through the jungle.

The most important factor in the successful use of the new force would be its supply from the air. The US Air Force organised a supply dropping routine second to none in the face of a powerful Japanese barrage from the ground and the air.

Merrill was then thirty-nine, a soldier who had risen through the ranks. He was short-sighted but this disability did nothing to dampen great determination. He had driven himself to win a place at West Point Military Academy, after failing the entrance examination five times. Gaining his commission he served for some time in cavalry regiments, then graduated with a Bachelor of Science degree at Massachusetts Institute of Technology. He gained one distinct advantage over many of his brother officers when in 1938 he was appointed Assistant Military Attaché in Tokyo. With his usual interest and enthusiasm he learned a great deal about the Japanese, their ways and their tactics in battle, from attending manoeuvres. It was to stand him in good stead.

Merrill was in Rangoon when the Japs struck and there he joined up with Stilwell and was with him throughout the retreat through Burma. He was then a major but he so impressed Stilwell with his enthusiasm and handling of affairs that his promotion was meteoric. Although this caused some envy among his fellow officers they had all to concede that the pipe-smoking ex-ranker was well liked by his subordinates, for ever friendly, confident and immensely enthusiastic.

By the end of January 1944, Merrill had whipped his force into battle readiness and they made their way to the front, there to gain the title that was to make them immortal – Merrill's Marauders. Stilwell described them as 'A tough lookin' lot o' babies'. They were to live up to that epithet in the fierce fighting that lay ahead.

The plan devised by Stilwell for the use of the Marauders was to give support to the advancing Chinese army by carrying out raids behind the Jap lines and in so doing dissipate the enemy forces. The conditions in which the Marauders were to fight were unbelievably grim. Indeed the terrain was often to prove a more formidable adversary than the enemy. They would be fighting on the western slopes and valleys of the mountains of north Burma. These precipitous slopes are densely overgrown with towering trees often reaching a hundred feet into the sky and forming a canopy of leaves and branches through which the sun cannot penetrate. At their base the ground is thick with fallen leaves and vegetation sometimes as much as four feet deep, making walking extremely difficult. It is no easier in the valleys where even in the clearings razor-sharp grass stands up to six feet high. Thick bamboo entwined with leaves and creepers form a barrier which has to be hacked away to make a path through it.

In winter the region becomes very cold and the chilled air produces a ground mist which makes navigation in the jungle extremely difficult. The puffy mist gives the Burmese landscape a ghostly, eerie hue. But when February comes the sun burns with growing intensity bringing intolerable humidity. Soon the country can take it no longer and the monsoon rains drown the land in a flood of water transforming narrow tracks into rivers of muddy sludge. It is almost continually damp in north Burma even in the dry season and the Marauders' weapons and metal equipment very quickly rusted if they were not oiled every day.

Disease ran rife among the 5307th. Few escaped malaria and dysentery. The jungle harboured an abundance of dangerous wild life; poisonous snakes, enormous buffalo flies, leeches, scrub typhus ticks, malarial mosquitoes and many others which sapped the strength from anyone who dared venture there. The leeches were a particular menace. Small and rubbery, they could attach themselves to a body without its owner knowing, particularly if he were asleep; then they would suck at his blood. Every Marauder's battledress was stained with blood where the leeches had been at work. An anti-coagulant in the leech's saliva made stemming the flow very difficult. But if the soldiers suffered, the mules fared even worse and they were invariably covered in blood. The open wounds attracted a fly which laid its eggs in the wounds and these hatched into ring worms.

The objective for the Chinese force was to drive the Japs back down the Kamaing Road. Two Chinese divisions supported by tanks began pushing down the road while the Marauders prepared to leave their assembly point at Ningbyen. Merrill's task was to swing to the east then turn in and cut off the Japanese retreat down the Kamaing Road. In addition he was to launch an attack against the Japanese command post situated near the Jambu Bum range of hills which straddled the road. Merrill was to use the Marauders in close cooperation with the main force, in contrast to Wingate's deep forages into the heart of Burma.

On 25 February 1944, the Marauders left their assembly point to go into battle for the first time as a complete force. They were not long in finding the war. An advance reconnaissance team sent out by Merrill to scout the area walked straight into a Jap ambush. Corporal Werner Katz, leading one of the scout teams, saw what he took to be Chinese soldiers waving to him. A few moments later the jungle exploded to the sound of machineguns. Katz dropped to the ground as bullets whipped through the air around him, ripping into the undergrowth and chipping the trees. He and the patrol had walked into the right flank of the Japanese positions. The exchange of fire was short and sharp and Katz survived the encounter with only a grazed nose. They now knew what they had been sent out to discover, the position of the Japanese, so they withdrew to report their find.

A few miles farther east another advance Marauder patrol, with Private Landis as lead scout, approached the village of Lanem Ga. There was a patch of clear ground immediately before the village and as the patrol crossed it, enemy guns in the village opened up. Landis fell dead, caught in the hail of fire, the first Marauder to be killed in Burma – the first of many. It was the following day before the others were able to recover his body. Such was the way of the fighting in the jungle.

Within the ranks of the Marauders were American Japanese, known as Nisei whose knowledge of the Japanese and their language was to be of inestimable value to the Marauders. In addition, the Marauders had other allies. They were the Kachins, natives of north Burma, who acted as guides and, under the direction of officers of the American Organization of Strategic Services, fought a guerrilla war against the Japanese. Their particular forte lay in ambushing the enemy. They knew the jungle better than anyone and could turn its danger to their advantage. The co-operation of the Kachins was gained in no small measure by the ministrations of a Roman Catholic priest, Father James Stuart, who had lived and worked with them for some time before the outbreak of war. By passing himself off to the Japs as Irish, he had avoided being taken prisoner and was allowed to continue living in peace with the Kachins. But his flock was far from peaceful and they gave the Japanese a very hard time. Many allied fliers owe their lives to the Kachins who rescued them after they had crashed in the jungle.

The first Marauder push into Burma went smoothly, the Japanese being unaware that there was a strong force cutting into the north of the country. By 3 March, the Marauders had received their last supply drop and were forging on towards their first objective, Walawbum, where they were to block the road. The terrain over which they were travelling was not too difficult and they managed to advance quite quickly, but they ran into a Japanese patrol and the fighting began in earnest. Thirty Japanese were killed. The Marauders then surged on and by the following day had established themselves in secure positions at Walawbum. But by then Tanaka, the Japanese commander, knew of their presence and resolved to wipe them out. If he did not, he would be squashed between the Marauders and the slowly advancing Chinese coming down the Kamaing Road. The Chinese were making slow progress so Tanaka left a small force to stem their advance while he moved the bulk of his forces down the road to sweep the Americans out of his line of escape.

When the Marauders established their positions they found that the Japanese telephone link between Tanaka's command post and the headquarters near Kamaing ran through their positions. The line was duly tapped and Sergeant Matsumoto was able to listen into the conversations and glean from them information which forewarned the Marauders of Tanaka's plans.

In the meantime, however, the Japanese were engaging in skirmishes with elements of the Marauder force in nearby areas. One of them was the combat team which carried the identifying name 'Khaki' and was protecting an area designated for a supply drop. The Jap attack came at dawn on 4 March. They cunningly used the early morning mist as a screen to hide their movements and with considerable skill succeeded in getting within a hundred yards of the Marauders' positions before they were discovered. Fighting almost blind in the mist, the Marauders accounted for ten Japanese before the enemy was forced to withdraw. But the score was to rise higher still. A group of Japs carrying one of their wounded got lost in the mist and walked straight into the 3rd Battalion's command post where they were cut down by small arms fire.

At Walawbum, the big fight opened when a strong enemy force clashed with the Marauders. Secure in their positions the Americans were able to bring their mortars and heavy machineguns to bear with lethal precision. The result was an estimated seventy Jap dead. On the debit side the Americans lost one man killed and seven wounded. So far the balance was in their favour.

Merrill, masterminding the Marauders' operation from a command post in the village of Wesu Ga, came close to becoming a casualty himself when Japanese machinegunners squirmed close to his headquarters. They might well have wiped it out had it not been for the lightning reactions of the defending Marauders who turned the tables and killed the lot.

Colonel Beach, the commander of the 3rd Marauder Battalion, also had a close shave when he was walking along a narrow trail to join up with one of his combat teams. Dense jungle flanked the trail and, as if from nowhere, a Japanese soldier stepped out of the undergrowth less than fifteen yards ahead of him. The Jap raised his rifle to fire but before he could pull the trigger, Beach's bodyguard felled him with a spray of bullets from his tommy gun.

The Japanese intensified their attacks on the American positions around Walawbum, mortaring them almost continuously. The Marauders retaliated by returning the mortar fire and calling up air strikes. One Marauder post suffered more than the others. It was at a point held by a small platoon of the 3rd Battalion, under the command of Lieutenant Weston. With suicidal determination the Japs launched five assaults on the platoon. They were fierce thrusts and might have been fatal had it not been for Sergeant Henry Gosho, the Japanese American 'Nisei' Marauder, who was with the platoon. He was able to interpret the yells of the Jap commanders as they led their men in the assaults and Weston could take appropriate defensive action. But each assault forced the Marauders to use up ammunition which was running short at an alarming rate. Furthermore, the accuracy of the Jap mortar fire was too good for comfort. Clearly if they remained there they would be slaughtered. Weston radioed his commander who ordered him to vacate his position. But to do so they had to cross an exposed river. A smoke screen was laid across the river which helped obscure the platoon as they carried their wounded through the swirling water. The Japs were bent upon annihilating Weston's platoon and they launched a fierce attack on the men in the river. Luckily a supporting Marauder team arrived on the bank they were heading for and they opened up on the Japs with mortars and small arms fire. One of them, Private Norman Janis, felled seven Japanese in the encounter. The Marauders successfully extricated themselves from the river and although they had been forced to withdraw they had wiped out at least two-thirds of the Jap force which had been attacking them, some sixty men.

The Japanese fought with equal vigour and determination against other elements of the Marauder force, notably the 2nd Battalion which was blocking the Kamaing Road west of Walawbum. The Japs swarmed

at the position in six vicious attacks throughout the
day while their artillery rained shells down on the
Americans. The clashes were bloody and costly, particularly for the Japanese who lost a hundred men
while the Americans suffered only six casualties. But the
severe Jap losses did nothing to stifle their determination. The barrage became so bad that the 2nd
Battalion's commander, Colonel McGee, decided that
the position must be vacated so that he could link up
with the 3rd Battalion. The Americans were not
the only ones to withdraw. Sergeant Matsumoto, tap-
ping the Jap communication line, discovered that a
general Jap withdrawal had been ordered. Now
McGee, by moving the 2nd Battalion to join the 3rd,
could all but completely block the Kamaing Road and
frustrate the Jap attempt at retreat.

The 2nd Battalion began moving out of their positions
at midnight and they did so with caution. Knowing the
Japanese propensity for booby traps they wisely drove a
mule ahead of the lead patrol as they slipped along the
trail. They had not gone far when the mule was blown
to bits. Tanaka knew that the Marauders dominated
the Kamaing Road and decided to pull his force west
and down a secondary track to avoid the road block.
The move was to bring about the bloodiest battle so far.

The battle opened at dawn on 6 March. While the
Japs fired a torrent of shells down on Merrill's command post to keep the Marauders' heads down during
their retreat, the two combat teams of the 3rd
Battalion, 'Orange' and 'Khaki', were subjected to
artillery and mortar fire against their position at a bend
in the Numpyek River. The Marauders had dug themselves in well and were secure behind stacked logs in
front of their fox holes. They replied to the Jap barrage
with mortar fire. Their accuracy was superb, owing to
Sergeant Andrew Pung who shinned up a tall tree and
directed the mortar fire from there. A projectile from
one of the mortars scored a direct hit on a truck laden

with Jap troops, killing them all. But Pung's position high up in that tree was extremely dangerous. A Jap shell exploded in the foliage, stripping it, shattering the tree and deafening the sergeant. He was lucky to get out alive and was stone deaf for more than a week.

It was clear to the Marauders that the barrage of fire was part of the softening up process before an assault, and sure enough, at 17.15 hours, the Japs came, two companies of them battling across the river towards the Marauders' stronghold. An earlier air strike had silenced some of the enemy artillery but not all of it and the shells continued to fall as the Jap infantry approached.

By then the Marauders were running desperately short of ammunition and they had to make every shot count. They held their fire while the Japs drew closer, wading through the swift-flowing current of water. The American mortars fired into the river and mighty spouts of water leapt into the air amid the advancing Japanese as the shells exploded. Yet the Japs forged on, goaded forward by sword-waving officers who were quick to administer violent persuasion to any soldier who dared hesitate in the advance.

When the two Jap companies had reached a point in the river about forty yards from the Americans, the Marauders opened up with machineguns and rifles. Two of the machineguns on the river bank had a clear field of fire and swept the river with bullets. Within seconds the river ran red with blood and bodies as the Japs were cut down. Four hundred Japs were massacred in that engagement. Not a single American was killed and only seven of them were wounded. The tattered remnants of the two Jap companies crawled back into the jungle. A few hours later, the Chinese entered Walawbum and secured it.

In that first phase of the operation, Merrill's Marauders had wiped out no fewer than eight hundred Japanese and, working in concert with the Chinese, pushed the Japs out of the Hukawng valley. This had been achieved at a cost to the Marauders of only eight men killed and thirty-seven wounded. But they had lost more to the jungle and disease than they had to the enemy, with 179 falling victim to one or other of them.

'Vinegar Joe' Stilwell was well pleased with the Marauders' performance and was justifiably proud of their showing in their first major tangle with the Japanese. Now he was to ask more of them. The engineers with their coolie labour were progressing well with the Burma road behind the Chinese. But now the gritty old commander wanted to push on.

The operation called for the Marauders to outflank the Japanese army on the Kamaing road and block it a little way south of the village of Shaduzup. The idea was to force Tanaka to vacate the Jambu Ridge, the range of hills which separated the Hukawng and Mogaung valleys. It was to be another sandwich operation and for it Stilwell decided to divide the Marauders into two forces. One of them, the 1st Battalion under Colonel Osborne, would move down the side of the Kamaing Road and set up the block at Shaduzup while the other two battalions would make a much wider arc east before turning in to block the road some ten miles south of the 1st Battalion.

Osborne's force moved out to begin their advance on 12 March and in the first two days made good progress, covering an amazing twenty miles over difficult terrain. They had brief brushes with the Japs but nothing of any great significance. They knew, however, that it could not last, and although they had covered twenty miles in only two days, it was to take them *two weeks* to reach their objective, only thirty miles farther on at Shaduzup. They walked straight into fierce Japanese opposition, so fierce that Osborne realised he could never hope to penetrate it along the narrow trail he was following. He was unaware that the rear of the Jap force was also under attack by Kachin guerrillas under the command of an American, Lieutenant Tilly. Had he known this, he might well have pressed on but instead he decided to cut a path through dense jungle to out-flank the enemy and try to keep to schedule for the block at Shaduzup.

The ground over which the 1st Battalion had to travel was the worst they had ever encountered. Dense undergrowth had to be cut away to take even one step. There were steep hills up which the mules could not carry the supplies and the packs had to be manhandled up the slopes. Progressing just a few yards was an exhausting trial and it took its toll of the Marauders. Almost all were affected by sickness and in particular dysentery which quickly sapped their already waning strength.

In a desperate state of fatigue they reached a point known as Kumshan Ga where they were to wait for an air drop. It came the day after they arrived, on 17 March, but because of the high surrounding hills, some of which reached 3000 feet, the aircraft had to make the drop from a great height. As a result, the supplies fell over a wide area and the men on the ground lost a whole day retrieving them.

They were allowed only brief respite and moved off again the following day. In the thirty-six hours that followed they advanced only four miles but the struggle had been worth it for at last they joined forces with the Kachins. These tribesmen were expert guides but there was a problem – the language. Only a few interpreters could understand the Kachins and the difficulty in communicating with them was to be highlighted shortly after they got underway again.

The Kachins were in the lead with a scouting patrol pushing through the jungle when they began whispering to the Americans in excited tones. The Marauders unfortunately mistook their chatter for requests for cigarettes or food. In fact they were warning them that there was a Jap ambush ahead. But it was too late. The

Japs opened fire, killing one Marauder and wounding two others. Luckily for the Marauders, the Japs had opened up too soon, firing before the Americans were properly ensnared in the trap, and other leading Marauders were able to flush out the ambushers and deal with them.

As the 1st Battalion moved on there were more encounters with the enemy, and it became clear the Marauders had stumbled into a large force of them. Osborne was forced to take another route to the Kamaing Road and they branched off the track. By 27 March they had reached the Chengun River and waded down it to reach its junction with the bigger Mogaung River. The point at which Osborne was to block the Kamaing Road was close to this junction.

Two of the reconnaissance team ahead, Lieutenant Wilson and Sergeant Tintary, were wading through the fast-flowing river near the junction when other members of the patrol on the bank warned them that there were Japanese soldiers on the opposite bank a little way ahead and moving towards them. The land ahead was teeming with them. The two Marauders were up to their necks in the water and the Jap patrol was bound to see them if they did not find cover on the bank. They only just managed to scramble on to dry land as the Japs passed. From their cover they watched as the Japs filled their water bottles from the river. Farther down-river were enemy soldiers casually fishing and bathing. It was a tranquil scene which clearly pointed to there being a strong Jap force in the area.

Wilson and Tintary crawled from the river bank to have a closer look at the Japanese camp. Between the river and the Kamaing Road they found the camp and estimated that there was at least company strength under canvas with considerable supplies of stores stacked high around the tents. Moving nearer to the road they found the camp unguarded and Japs casually wandering around on the other side.

The two Marauders made their way back to the river and upstream to Osborne. When the colonel heard of their find, he resolved to launch an attack at dawn the following day. The Marauders would sweep through the camp and establish the road block afterwards. 'White' Combat Team was selected for the attack with 'Red' Combat Team covering.

Just before dawn three Marauder platoons slipped across the river, with three more platoons close behind in reserve. With the first rays of daylight, the Japanese camp stirred. Men crawled sleepily out of their tents to attend to their personal toilet. Then the hammerblow struck. The jungle reverberated to the crack of rifle fire and the rasp of machineguns as the Japs were mown down, while other Marauders used their bayonets. Hand grenades burst and fragmented among the enemy, killing and maiming.

Complete surprise had been achieved and the numbed Japs did not have a chance against the onslaught. Lieutenant Caldwell's platoon was the first to reach the road and they quickly set up a block. Shortly after, a Jap truck sped down the road and into a hail of fire which wiped out the three-man crew.

When the Japs collected their wits, they returned the American fire and an artillery barrage was directed at the newly-established American positions. This lasted throughout the day and the following night, but there was no shifting the Marauders. For the second time the Japs found themselves being squeezed between the Americans and the Chinese. The vice was closing on them but they fought tenaciously until they were overwhelmed and the Chinese occupied Shaduzup. At last the hard-pressed Marauders were relieved and able to vacate the area for some rest. They had lost eight men killed and thirty-five wounded in a valiant action. But, to the east, things were going very badly for the Marauders of the 2nd and 3rd Battalions. Osborne's force received an urgent call for help.

The 2nd and 3rd Battalions had faired well during the opening stages of their move south. It had begun on 12 March and took them down the valley of the Tanai River. By comparison with their comrades in the 1st Battalion they made excellent time, pausing only to take an air drop then moving on again. On 15 March they joined forces with a 300-strong band of Kachin guerrillas under the command of an American, Captain Vincent Curl. They were a motley bunch, ranging in age from twelve to sixty but they had shown themselves to be good fighters and were a welcome addition to the Marauder force.

The combined force reached the town of Janpan on 19 March after a tough day's trek up a precipitous trail. The following day Merrill got news of a 2000-strong Japanese force to the south-west of Kamaing. Such a force would pose a considerable threat to his plan to block the Kamaing Road at Inkangahtawng. To cope with the opposition Merrill split the Marauders, assigning McGee's 2nd Battalion and the 'Khaki' Combat Team of 3rd Battalion to reconnoitre the tracks leading to the Japanese base at Kamaing then move west to block the road. In the meantime 'Orange' Combat Team of the 3rd Battalion was to carry out reconnaissance to the south and west of Janpan.

The following day McGee's force left Janpan and marched the fourteen miles to Auche where there was a change of plan. Merrill ordered them to make directly for the road block and they turned west. In the meantime 'Orange' Combat Team was sent to block off the trail leading up from the south towards Auche.

In the course of the first part of their trek west, McGee's Marauders were obliged to cross and recross a river no fewer than fifty-six times in less than eight miles. The going was difficult but the Marauders could cope and despite a brush with the Japanese the 2nd Battalion established the road block on the evening of 23 March. But the Japs were up to something. From their positions the Americans could hear movement on the road near by. When patrols were sent out to scout the area they found their way blocked by strong Jap forces. In fact the enemy was massing to launch an all-out attack upon the Marauders at Inkangahtawng.

The Marauders dug themselves in as the Jap mortar shells fell on their position. Their assessment of the situation was made more difficult because their view was restricted by towering grass. They could hear the Japs but could not see them. It was frustrating – and dangerous.

When the barrage of mortar fire lifted the confused battle cries of the Japs could be heard. The enemy struggled through the long grass until, only twenty yards from the Americans, they came into view. From their fox-holes the Marauders opened up at almost point blank range, killing many of the enemy before they could make much headway. Those who did get farther were smartly dealt with.

It will be remembered that at this point the 1st Battalion had not yet reached Shaduzup so that the Japanese were able to concentrate on demolishing McGee's force. In the first twenty-four hours, they launched sixteen assaults against the 1st Battalion's positions. When the Jap infantry was not attacking, their gunners were laying a barrage of artillery and mortar fire. McGee called in the air force to straff and bomb the enemy but there was little let up in their attacks. Jap reinforcements were brought forward to add weight to the onslaught and by the end of the first day the outlook was decidedly grim for the Marauders. Ammunition was low and there was little hope of the Chinese army advancing with any speed to relieve the situation. In addition to this, McGee learned that two Jap battalions were moving north from Kamaing up the banks of the Tanai River. Taking these things into account, McGee sensibly decided to withdraw. He could see that he would be needed to counter the threat of the north-bound Japs. He had already killed some two hundred Japs at the road block for the loss of two men killed and twelve wounded. It was pointless holding the road block position with the Chinese so far north.

When Merrill heard of the Japanese advance north from Kamaing, he ordered the 2nd and 3rd Battalions to block the main trail at Nhpum Ga. While they made their way to take up these defensive positions there was bitter fighting between the Marauders in the south and the advancing Japs. The small Marauder unit comprised of only two platoons was given the hopeless task of holding up the advance of some eight hundred Japanese troops. Using ambush techniques on the narrow trails they subtracted a number of Japs from the force but there was no halting the inexorable advance of the enemy. The crucial factor was to establish a firm hold in the trail north of its junction at Auche, and the 2nd and 3rd Battalions were moving to do just that.

The battle-weary, sick and bedraggled men of the two battalions fought their way through the jungle and after a tortuous trek reached Auche on the 27th. They had covered seventy miles over the past few days, wading knee and neck deep in rivers and thrashing their way through thick jungle. Had it not been for the Marauders in the two platoons delaying the Japanese, they would never have made it in time. The men of the two platoons, ninety of them in all, had killed around sixty Japanese without a single loss of life to themselves.

The 3rd Battalion carried on towards Nhpum Ga while the 2nd Battalion set up a defensive perimeter at Auche to hold the fort and allow as many men of the 3rd to reach Nhpum Ga as was possible. The following day they too moved out of Auche but by now the Japs had brought their artillery into play and they pounded the area, finding the Marauders' range with devastating accuracy. Shell shock was commonplace as the missiles ravaged the jungle trail, taking their toll of men and animals who fought up the steep incline towards Nhpum Ga. The track was covered in deep squelching mud. They slid and fell as they went, falling into the ooze and often too exhausted to pull themselves up. It happened time and time again. The mules suffered too for they fell more often and when they did they had to be unloaded before they could be righted again. The mental agony was such that some men could take it no longer. They had reached their breaking point and threw away their equipment. Some charged half crazed into the jungle, anywhere to get away from the hell of the bombardment. Their comrades, themselves near to breaking, rescued them and did their best to soothe their shattered nerves.

By 22.00 hours the bulk of the Marauders had reached Nhpum Ga. The stream of men who struggled up that hill was a pathetic sight, their faces gaunt and grey. Some screamed at the tops of their voices in demented torment at the crashing shells that continued to fall around them.

Despite their wretched condition, the Marauders set to fortifying the twin hill top that was Nhpum Ga. From there they hoped to halt the Japanese advance. The events that were about to be enacted at this remote spot in north Burma were to test the men's endurance to the absolute limit in a siege that stands as one of the most valiant moments in American military history.

It fell to the 2nd Battalion to hold Nhpum Ga. Holding this hill-top vantage point was critical, not only because it dominated the surrounding countryside but because from there the Marauders could prevent the Japs by-passing it and attacking the flank of the south-bound Chinese army. Furthermore, there was a vital air strip near by to which supplies could be flown in, and from which sick and wounded soldiers were evacuated. That had to be held and if Nhpum Ga fell, the air strip was certain to fall too. So McGee and the 2nd Battalion had a formidable responsibility. If they succumbed

Stilwell's Burmese campaign might crumble.

On the credit side they were well placed, some 2800 feet high. By carefully sighting his defensive perimeter, McGee had the only water hole in the area. But on the debit side, his men were in no condition to combat a determined offensive from the Japanese which the Japs lost no time in launching. The barrage lasted for almost four hours, directed mainly at the Marauder rearguard about a mile south of Nhpum Ga. Unable to take it any longer the rearguard joined the rest of the Battalion. In the meanwhile the 3rd Battalion had moved out to guard the air strip. Now the Japs brought the full weight of their artillery to bear on Nhpum Ga, saturating the area with shells.

For the next two days the 2nd and 3rd Battalions remained in contact with each other by sending out patrols, but on 30 March one of the patrols was badly mauled by the Japs. From the next day onwards, Nhpum Ga was cut off. McGee's battalion was alone . . .

To the men in the fox-holes it felt as if the entire Japanese army was bombarding their stronghold, while at every point along the 400-yard perimeter Jap assault squads kept up almost continuous raids. High velocity guns shelled the area at point blank range making it impossible for the Marauders to predict when a shell would hit. No sooner had the crash of the gun reached their ears than the shell would land. There was no time to duck or take cover. The Marauders were virtually confined to their fox-holes. And there was another menace. The Japs had posted snipers around the American perimeter and anything that moved on the exposed hill crests got a bullet. When night fell the snipers kept up their fire, firing in the direction of the slightest sound. The Marauders became prisoners, not daring to leave their fox-holes. One of them tried and was shot, not by a sniper, but by one of his own men who mistook him for an enemy. To venture out of the dubious sanctuary of the fox-hole was courting death. They were forced to use their helmets to relieve themselves with the result that their prison stank; a noxious, sickening stench of urine and waste which made them retch. It was made worse by the dreadful odour coming from dead mules. These animals had been killed in the shelling and because of the Jap fire the Marauders could not get to them to bury them. In the heat of the day, the dead animals had swollen and their decomposing flesh, infested with flies, added its own potency to the smell.

A further setback came for the Marauders when the Japanese overran the waterhole. Now the besieged troops had no fresh water. Then came the news that the Japs had taken the track between them and the 3rd Battalion. Their dwindling morale took another dive. Rescue from their plight now seemed impossible.

The shelling did not let up and it strained the sanity of the men. Marauders had died and lay unburied. By 1 April seven had been lost and another twenty-five wounded, as well as almost a hundred mules. But the Japs had not had it all their own way. Despite the terrible privations, the Marauders had held their perimeter and kept up the fight. The area around their position was strewn with some two hundred Japanese dead.

As the hours passed the Marauders' condition grew worse. Without water they were forced to drink the thick muddy ooze at the bottom of their fox-holes. None of them had the stomach for food. They were desperate, particularly for water, and McGee called the air force for a supply drop of water. Then on 2 April the heavens opened and they were able to collect a little palatable rain water. The following day the air drop came and with that a lift in their spirits. Good news arrived when they learned that the 1st Battalion had secured Shaduzup.

The Japanese who were attacking Nhpum Ga were in desperate straits too. They had lost many more men than the Marauders and were as vulnerable to the privations of the jungle as the Americans. In one incident a Jap soldier wandered into the American lines, clearly not knowing where he was. Half crazed he stumbled forward until an American bullet put him out of his misery.

There were many instances of selfless courage on that hill-top but that of Sergeant Roy Matsumoto, the Japanese American, must rank among the greatest. Night after night he left his fox-hole and slid into the Japanese lines where he listened to the conversations of the officers and men, then he made his way back to the Americans with his store of intelligence.

Matsumoto's own fox-hole was situated at the point of a spur on the Marauders' perimeter. One night when he reached the Jap lines he learned that the enemy was to attack that spur at dawn the following morning. When he told his lieutenant of the impending raid a possibility was seen of surprising the raiders. Lieutenant McLogan withdrew his men from the fox-holes to positions higher up the hill, having first planted booby traps in the fox-holes they had vacated. Then they waited.

Dawn seemed to be an eternity in coming. Then as the sky to the east brightened the Japanese rushed up the hill, just as Matsumoto had predicted. Yelling and shouting damnation to the Americans they swamped the American trenches. Their 'victory' was swift and the officers at their head urged them on to take more American-held land. Not a shot had been fired by the Marauders. Then when the Japs were within fifty feet of them McLogan and his men let loose a withering hail of fire. The Japs were cut down by the weight of bullets thrashing into them. Those who escaped the wall of bullets leapt into the booby-trapped trenches and triggered off the explosives. The slope in front of the Marauders' positions was a graveyard of dead and dying Japanese but they were not finished. There were reserves at the foot of the hill waiting to fill the gaps.

Matsumoto knew this and yelled in Japanese, 'Charge! Charge!' They obeyed and launched themselves into the full fury of the American guns. By the time the Japanese finally gave up the attack they had lost fifty-four men dead. But the victory did nothing to lessen the Marauders' desperate situation.

North of Nhpum Ga the 3rd Battalion was making a brave attempt to break through and rescue the 2nd Battalion from the siege. The task facing them was incredibly difficult. Merrill had been taken ill and had handed over temporary command to Colonel Hunter. He knew that if he did not break the siege soon the Japs would throttle the 2nd Battalion out of existence. The forces capable of effecting a relief were themselves engaged in heavy fighting and the 1st Battalion was four days' march away. Hunter planned a series of thrusts to break through the Jap lines. The trails to Nhpum Ga were blocked by strong units of Japanese and he knew that the cost of the relief was likely to be high.

The main assault was launched by 3rd Battalion in the late afternoon of 4 April. Diversionary attacks, air strikes and artillery barrages paved the way, then the battalion began its push. It was a bloody encounter, but the American initiative paid off and they got within a thousand yards of Nhpum Ga.

Although the battle did much to hearten the prisoners of Nhpum Ga, they feared that they would not be able to hold out until the 3rd Battalion got through. On the night before the battle three of their wounded had died. One Marauder lay outside the perimeter with the front of his skull shot off, exposing his brain. The Marauders tried to rescue him but enemy fire held them back. It was not until a lull in the fighting after dawn that they managed to get him into a foxhole where he died later that morning.

The Japs continued probing the perimeter and at one point managed to penetrate it but were pushed back again. That night they tried a repeat operation but Matsumoto had already paid a visit to their lines and they were expected.

Nothing changed for two days. The enemy was still bent on taking Nhpum Ga despite Hunter's push from the north. On the narrow trails they fought for every inch of ground, slowing up the progress of Hunter's relief force. The tracks were so narrow that only two platoons of Marauders could lead the fight. As they gained ground they saw what the Japanese had suffered. The area had been ravaged by artillery fire and bombs. At one position they found the trees hanging with Jap bodies, cast there by bomb blasts.

On 6 April, McGee counted his casualties. He had lost seventeen men killed, four were missing and about a hundred were wounded. Those who were not seriously wounded remained in their fox-holes to keep up the defence.

Then on 7 April McGee, knowing that the leading element of the relief force was only 500 yards away, decided to launch a break out to link up with it. It failed, but then Osborne's 1st Battalion arrived to reinforce the struggling 3rd. The combined force could now launch its assault with greater strength. On the 8th, however, they were virtually halted, despite heavy air and artillery attacks on the Japs. On 9 April, Easter Sunday, with the awful stench permeating through the jungle to them, Osborne's 1st Battalion fought its way along a trail to the west of Nhpum Ga and from there round the hills along which the Japs had moved and had positions. To their amazement they found it empty. Equipment was littered all over the place, fires still smouldered. Edging cautiously along the track they realised that the Japs had fled. They quickened their pace along the track towards Nhpum Ga – and walked in without resistance.

To the north the 3rd Battalion flushed away the last of the Japs and they too reached the hill crests where the 2nd Battalion had been under siege for ten long, hellish days.

None of the rescuers was prepared for the horror that confronted them when they reached the hill tops. There were dead, grotesquely bloated mules lying about the devastated area. Among them were dead men, American and Japanese. Shadowy figures emerged from fox-holes to meet the men who had rescued them. For some the rescue had come too late.

In that awful siege the 2nd Battalion lost just twenty-five men and a little over a hundred wounded while the Japanese suffered four hundred killed.

The Marauders went on to take part in the eventual recapture of Burma displaying the same heroism they had shown in the trying and testing thrust from the north. But no episode in their short history can match the siege of Nhpum Ga for sheer guts and heroism. 'Vinegar Joe' got his Burma road, thanks to the valour and self-sacrifice of 'a tough lookin' lot o' babies' – Merrill's Marauders.

3

Air Sea Rescue

The Bay of Biscay was in malevolent mood that night of 12 August 1942. An hour before dawn it was still dark with dense cloud shrouding the moon. A strong wind swept the sea's surface, shredding the crests off the wave tops and casting a misty spray into the air. A symphony of howling sound was accompanied by the dull throb of engines. An intruder probed the night, forcing its way through the weather, a thousand feet above the sea and just beneath the low cloud base. The twin-engined Wellington bomber, nursed through the air by an RAF crew, followed an invisible track along a straight line over the sea then altered course along another, predetermined path. She was a predator, hunting a quarry that hid beneath the waves. Her prey was U-boats of the German *Kriegsmarine* slipping in and out of France's Atlantic ports. These vessels posed the greatest possible threat to Britain's survival of the war.

The Bay was the launching point of Germany's war upon the ships that plied the Atlantic convoy routes, ferrying the vital supplies of munitions and food to beleaguered Britain. From Brest and St Nazaire, among other ports, U-boats lanced out into the Atlantic and brought havoc to the convoys, sinking millions of tons of shipping. Admiral Karl Doenitz, architect of the U-boat war, knew he could strangle Britain into defeat. Deprived of the victuals to feed the war machine, Britain would grind to a halt and succumb.

The Royal Navy, determined to plug the U-boats'
exit to the Atlantic from the Biscay bases, patrolled the
Bay in order to catch and destroy the enemy submarines
as they left port or returned from their patrols. But that
was not enough. The RAF mounted airborne patrols
over the Bay using a variety of bomber aircraft
equipped with radar search equipment for detecting
the U-boats and depth charges for attacking them when
they were found.

The Wellington bomber, nicknamed the 'Wimpey',
played a crucial role in these anti-submarine patrols. In
the early part of the war, the Wimpey was the mainstay
of RAF bomber command until the introduction of the
four-engined heavy bombers. She was a sturdy aircraft
with a fuselage of geodetic construction, built up of a
lattice work of short pieces of pressed steel bolted
together to form a sort of basket. This form of construction was developed by the makers, Vickers, from their
work on the airship R100. In its role as a bomber the
Wimpey had a range of around 1400 miles and could
carry a bomb-load of 4500 pounds. She was armed with
six machineguns, two in a nose turret and four in a
rear turret in the tail. But when engaged in anti-
submarine operations the Wimpey had to be modified.
The nose turret was removed and replaced by a Leigh
light, a powerful searchlight which could be switched
on for night attacks. Its beam could light up the sea for
almost a mile. Housed in the after part of the fuselage
was the search radar, a mass of equipment which could
uncover a submarine no matter what the weather; a
potent weapon in the fight against the U-boats.

For the crews of the Wellingtons, the anti-submarine
patrols were invariably long and tedious. They flew for
hour upon hour over the vast area of unchanging sea,
rarely making contact with enemy submarines. Night
sorties were especially taxing. The men had to struggle
against boredom and yet remain alert for the moment
when a U-boat might be betrayed on the radar screen.

That particular night followed the pattern of so many the Wellington's crew had experienced in the past. No contacts were made with enemy vessels. They longed for the first rays of dawn that would signal the time to head for home; back to a hot breakfast and the carefree oblivion of sleep. But throughout the long hours of the patrol every man had been haunted by the uneasy feeling that all was not well. Flying Officer Triggs, the Wimpey's skipper, had detected it not long after he took off from Chivenor, near Barnstaple, in Devon. The aircraft's engines had not had their familiar, comfortable drone. They were off-key and, although his instruments showed no cause for alarm, Triggs had been tempted to return to base. After due deliberation, however, he resolved to carry on. But the thought that trouble lay ahead would not leave him.

Triggs, an Australian, tried his best to hide that uneasiness from his crew but they too felt a sense of foreboding. Pilot Officer Devonshire, sitting remote from the rest of the crew in the rear turret, was no exception. He pondered upon what had brought him thousands of miles from his native Canada to this inhospitable region as he scanned the sky for marauding enemy aircraft.

Anxiety was felt too by Pilot Officer Badham, another Australian and the aircraft's navigator. Flight Sergeant McLean, the radar operator who sat with his set waiting for the sign on the screen that would expose an enemy submarine, felt similarly disturbed, as did Sergeant Walker, Triggs' co-pilot, and Cartwright, the wireless operator. All of them were edgy and tense.

The first hint that their premonitions of trouble might come true came about an hour before dawn. It was Devonshire who spotted the sparks trailing out behind the aircraft. They were spewing out of the starboard engine and he immediately called Triggs on the intercom.

Triggs recognised the unmistakable Canadian drawl. 'How bad?'

'Bad enough and getting worse,' Devonshire warned.

Triggs' reaction was immediate. His hand darted to the throttle and his eyes to the oil pressure gauge. Already it was falling fast and in moments it had reached zero. The starboard motor spluttered and coughed as it was starved of oil, its note now hoarse and rough. Triggs pulled back on the throttle, reducing the power on the ailing motor and compensated for the loss of power by applying starboard rudder. For a few moments the Wellington remained on an even keel but the arteries of the engine were running dry. The engine gave a deep-throated bronchial cough then fell silent. The three-bladed propeller stopped its spin and stood rigid. Triggs cut its fuel supply lessening the chance of fire.

The Wimpey was now lame, kept airborne by the port engine. She was far from home, too far to limp back. Triggs realised then that they would never make it home. They would have to ditch but he resolved to get as close to home as possible before putting her down in the sea. He set course for the south of England. The crew began preparing themselves for the inevitable, Badham plotting their exact position while Cartwright began sending out distress signals but the aircraft had lost height and Cartwright feared that she was too low for the signal to be heard by friendly ears.

The port engine complained with an agonising wail as it struggled to keep the aircraft airborne. Triggs knew that he was fighting a losing battle. The temperature on the port engine was rising alarmingly and it could only be a matter of time before it too gave out.

'Not long now,' he thought, switching on his intercom. 'Get rid of everything you can, anything that's movable or that you can rip out and chuck overboard. We've got to lighten her. Parachutes – the lot. We're not going to need chutes where we're going. I'll ditch the depth charges. Make it snappy. We're running out of time.'

The crew began cannibalising the Wimpey while Triggs released the depth charges. But it was a futile struggle. The Wimpey continued to sink.

Triggs waged war on the control column, trying to keep her in the air for a few more minutes.

'It's no good,' he told the crew. 'Hasn't made a blind bit of difference. Stand by to ditch. I'm going to put her down soon. We'll get our feet wet but we should be okay. Badham, which way's the wind blowing?'

'Two eight zero degrees true, Skipper,' Badham replied, having predicted Triggs' request. 'Wind speed about thirty knots. But watch it, there's quite a swell on down there. The waves are breaking about three feet high and running down wind with the swell. The sea's swelling to about twenty feet with the crests about a couple of hundred yards apart.'

The ever-reliable Badham had given him all the information he could to help him put the Wimpey down in the sea. The rest was up to him, and his judgement could mean the difference between life and death for him and the rest of the crew.

His mind worked like lightning racing in urgent calculations to decide how he was to do it and it was beset with considerable problems. The specially modified Wimpey had a tendency to be tail heavy because of the absence of the nose turret and the mass of radar equipment in the after part of the fuselage. This, coupled with the plane's inclination to swerve because of flying on only one engine was to make ditching a supreme test of his skill. He was particularly concerned about the very real possibility of the aircraft breaking up and bursting into flames on impact with the water. She was still carrying a great deal of fuel in her wing tanks and the safest bet would be to get rid of as much of it as possible before putting her down in the sea. He reckoned he could hang on long enough for that but even this posed a problem. It would accentuate the tail-heavy attitude of the plane by lightening the wings. If he did that and landed with the tail hitting the water first, the Wimpey might break her back. But there was no time to argue the pros and cons with himself and he decided to keep the fuel on board.

There were two alternatives open to Triggs. He could land into the wind but this meant he might strike the waves head on and plunge straight underwater. Or he could put her down in a trough between the waves by landing across wind. The danger there lay in the Wimpey slewing and tipping over. With one engine out of order and as a consequence the Wimpey inclining to slew to port, he felt it too dangerous and thought it wiser to land into wind and risk the possibility of going under.

By now the remainder of the crew were in their ditching positions and braced for the impact that was about to come. It was all up to Triggs now.

The sea below was a hazy, dark void and when Triggs read the radio altimeter, it showed only a hundred feet of air space between him and the water. He switched on the Leigh light and the cone of light lit up the sea. It appeared to be in a turmoil and much closer than he imagined. At fifty feet the aircraft was buffeted by the turbulence and spray lashed the Wellington. Triggs struggled with the controls to keep her on an even keel as the swirling wind caught her surfaces and tried to force her into a fatal gyration. At thirty feet, Triggs hauled the aircraft round into the wind. It bolted across the wave tops as he strained to hold her off at seventy knots. He could feel the tail sinking lower and the nose rising out of his control.

The tail was the first to hit and it slammed into the water, jarring the aircraft and dragging the remainder of the plane down into the sea with it. Triggs had done his best and in an instant the Wimpey sliced through a wave. The sea gushed in through the open emergency hatches flooding the inside of the fuselage and then all was still. The sea had finally arrested her in her dash. Mercifully she was intact but was taking in water fast.

Triggs' first concern was for the fate of his crew. He was still in one piece, having been held in position by his harness but by now the water was up to his waist and still pouring in. By some miracle, none of the crew was seriously injured in the crash. Cartwright had been thrust forward and cut an eye but he was still conscious and able to help McLean through the escape hatch and scramble out himself.

Triggs undid his safety harness and got out of his seat but his foot trod upon something soft on the floor. He felt down into the water and pulled. It was Walker his co-pilot. He'd been knocked unconscious when the aircraft hit. Triggs hauled him out of the water and summoned his strength to push him through the escape hatch above them, then he too scrambled out and pulled Walker's limp body on to the top of the fuselage.

In the tail, Devonshire escaped by rotating the turret and wriggling free. Meanwhile Badham, the only man left inside the fuselage, pulled at the dinghy release but a yell from outside told him that it had not come free. To add further to the tension of the moment, someone outside shouted to tell him that the emergency ration pack was missing. Badham thought he had seen it in the confusion immediately after the crash and set about finding it. At last he found it and tossed it out to Cartwright who reminded him that the dinghy was still not released. Badham courageously returned to the release handle with the thought constantly in his mind that if the aircraft were to go down now, he would go with it. The water was rising quickly as he grappled for the release and gave it an almighty tug but it was hopeless. Outside on the wing, Cartwright fought to get the dinghy out by pulling the manual release. Try as he might, it would not budge. All the time the aircraft was sinking lower into the sea, increasing the possibility that they would lose the dinghy altogether and find themselves floating in the water. McLean came to Cartwright's aid but their struggle was in vain. Then Triggs put his bare hands to the stowage and managed to wrench it free, releasing the dinghy. It hissed as it inflated and all the crew, including Badham, clambered aboard but they quickly realised that they did not have the emergency pack. It had been left on the wing. One of them spotted it and it was retrieved.

By now only the top of the fuselage and the tail stuck up above the surface of the water. The landing lights which were still shining beneath the surface gave the whole scene a ghostly hue. The five men, wet through, huddled together in the dinghy. Fierce bouts of sea-sickness caught each one of them as the dinghy was tossed about like a cork on the sea. Their stomachs retched and they vomited into the well of the dinghy. They set about baling out the cocktail of vomit and sea but it was a half-hearted attempt. Gradually, however, after almost two hours of baling they began to make an impression upon the waterlogged dinghy and the level dropped. The thought that their efforts were paying off gave them their first vestige of new heart, but even so, none of them knew if McLean's radio transmission had reached their base.

They had been due back at Chivenor at 05.30 hours and when they failed to arrive the station would be put on the alert. But, with the weather the way it was, there seemed to be little chance of their being spotted from the air. On the credit side, they did have the dinghy and as time passed they managed to scoop out all the water from the well. They had an adequate supply of food and water and Triggs estimated that, with rationing, they had enough to last for several days.

Of them all, Triggs and Badham were first to show the will to fight and give a hint of optimism. By now search aircraft would be taking off to look for them. Dawn had come and although it was a grey, dismal day, it helped boost their morale. By now they had got over the first awful bout of sea-sickness. Now they could at least see their enemy, a forbidding, desolate sea which would give them little respite.

What conversation there was centred on the prospect of rescue. There was a possibility they might be picked up by French fishermen who were known to fish that area. They estimated that they were about eighty or ninety miles off the French coast and their nearest landfall would be Brest. If their calculations were correct then the British anti-submarine patrols would pass their way. The less confident of them pointed out that there was also a damned good chance of being spotted by the Luftwaffe whose aircraft patrolled the Bay in search of RAF and RN patrols. Rumour had it that German pilots were not averse to shooting up survivors in dinghies.

Badham concentrated upon navigational calculations. He judged that they were some 180 miles from England. This, coupled with their close proximity to the French coast, made it unlikely that the rescue services would chance sending out launches to pick them up. It was a gloomy thought. But then, as Badham was working out a course to narrow the gap between them and England, one of them let out a yell.

'A Wimpey! Look!' His finger pointed towards the unmistakable shape of a Wellington droning across the Bay about a mile from their position. They agreed that it was probably one of their own squadron en route for its patrol area. There was little hope of its crew spotting the minute dinghy from that distance. They did have two distress rockets but they jointly decided to save them for when there was a better chance of being seen. Soon the aircraft was a mere speck in the distance and then it disappeared.

They watched the sky in the hope that they might see another aircraft. A strong wind whipped up the sea and

a biting spray lashed their faces. It stung their eyes,
coated their faces in white salt and found its way into
their mouths.

Minutes dragged by like hours. Surely by now the alarm
must have been raised – but why no searching aircraft?
Perhaps they had been given up for lost.

It was shortly after 08.30 hours when one of them
caught sight of the aircraft bolting over the sea not far
off. It was a Beaufighter and it was coming closer. It
would, if it remained on course, pass within a quarter of
a mile. Triggs grabbed one of the two distress rockets
and prepared to fire it when the aircraft was at its
closest point. The Beaufighter was low over the water,
too low to be on patrol. It had to be searching for them.
They prayed that it would not alter course before
Triggs fired the rocket.

The Beaufighter was soon less than a quarter of a
mile distant. Triggs lifted the distress flare and fired.
Instantly the rocket soared skyward and lit in a brilliant burst. It arched lazily as it reached the apex of its
flight then floated gently towards the grey sea. The
Beaufighter sped on clinging to its course.

'It's no use,' one of them said. 'They haven't seen us!'

'Blind bastards!' another mouthed in a curse he did
not mean. He knew how difficult it was to see a flare in
the conditions that prevailed. But their deteriorating
morale made it difficult to be understanding.

The general consensus of opinion was that the
Beaufighter had indeed been searching for them. Why
otherwise would it have been flying so low? And there
was some consolation in the knowledge that a search had
been mounted. But now they had only one rocket left and
Triggs dared not use it unless it was an absolute certainty
that they would be seen. Without a rocket to point their
position, it would be a miracle if they were seen at all.
A dinghy was a very small craft to see from an aircraft.

Triggs and the redoubtable Badham knew that their
greatest enemy was despair. If they allowed themselves

to give up hope they would surely be lost. Both of them resolved to do all they could to raise the spirits of the men. They joked and sang and the pantomime worked.

As the morning progressed and the day lightened, the weather improved and so too did their prospects of rescue as more aircraft were seen. Several of them came within sighting distance and one of them, a Whitley bomber, skimmed across the sea so close that they felt sure they must have been seen. Triggs thought that then was the time to fire their last rocket but as it burst above the dinghy the Whitley charged on without noticing it.

None of the ten aircraft they saw that morning spotted them. Badham suggested erecting a sail. If the aircraft searching for them could not find them then they must make an effort to reach land.

Badham's crudely fashioned sail did seem to make an impression upon the dinghy's progress and he was able to direct the craft towards the French coast. They resigned themselves to the thought that capture was preferable to a watery grave, and the gap narrowed between them and France.

Noon came and went and it was early afternoon when they saw aircraft coming their way. They were recognisable as a Whitley bomber escorted by Beaufighters. Anxiously the men in the dinghy waved a flag to attract the attention of the crews and dipped a fluorescein bag in the water. The bag contained a dye which stained the water to help the searchers find them. It worked.

The aircraft altered course and soared towards them. Now surely, they thought, it must be only a matter of time before they were picked up. None of them at that moment considered how it was to be done. They were too overjoyed at having been found.

The Whitley bomber roared over their heads and the pilot dipped his wings, indicating that he had seen the dinghy. They cheered with delight as the bomber circled the dinghy while the Beaufighters buzzed high overhead keeping watch for marauding German air-craft. After a few circuits, the Whitley dropped her nose and began a long, slow run-in over the dinghy. Her bomb bay opened and a dinghy dropped from the air-craft. It hurtled seaward and landed with a splash upwind of the stricken crew. Triggs and the others bent themselves to the paddles and made a valiant attempt to reach the other dinghy – but it was a hopeless task. The sea forced them back with every stroke. But the pilot of the Whitley saw their predicament and flew over them once more, this time dropping a bag of sup-plies a little downwind of Triggs' dinghy. The floating bag bobbed on the sea and they reversed course to retrieve it. All of them now felt confident that they would soon be home and dry. But as the Whitley and the Beaufighters winged their way back towards England, the thought was not lost upon them that pick-ing them up would be difficult.

In the bag they found a supply of food as well as a Very pistol and cartridges. At least they would now be able to signal their position when other aircraft arrived.

Half an hour later another Whitley appeared. Triggs fired the Very pistol and within minutes the Whitley was circling overhead with its signal lamp flashing. McLean read off the morse code message. It told them that a Sunderland flying boat would be coming to pick them up. With that the Whitley departed, leaving them alone with their thoughts.

The flying boat arrived just as the light was beginning to fade. A Very cartridge pin-pointed their position to the crew of the cumbersome Sunderland. The great aeroplane laboriously heaved itself round and headed for the dinghy. The four-engined flying boat roared as it swept over them and dropped a wing to circle them. Triggs looked at the waves which rose above the dinghy then up at the aircraft. No, he thought, there was no chance of the pilot's attempting a landing. It was much too dangerous.

After all, he had his own crew to think of. There would always be tomorrow.

The Sunderland levelled out and set course away from the dinghy, while the men in the dinghy watched with sinking hearts. It was a bitter disappointment. What they would have given to be inside the flying boat drinking down hot coffee and pulling on a cigarette. But now they would have to endure another night in the Bay.

It was then that the shock of explosions and the eruption of the sea beneath the Sunderland jolted them. For a moment they could not understand what was happening. Then they realised that the flying boat was dropping depth charges. At first they imagined that the Sunderland crew had spotted a U-boat and were attacking but then it became clear that she was ditching her depth charges before making an attempt at landing.

The flying boat was about a mile from the dinghy when she began to lose height and dipped towards the sea in a gentle descent. The crew in the dinghy sat tight-lipped, willing her down safely. Soon she was only a few feet above the waves.

She was almost there, lashed by the spray and then her shaped hull touched the crest of the first wave. It cut through it but between it and the next one was a deep trough. The Sunderland had the bare minimum of power on, too little for a change of mind. The point of no return had been reached and the flying boat lingered on stalling speed. Then she stalled, hit the crest of the swell, smashed into a wave, glanced off that and charged into another, hitting it like a ricochet. She lurched nose up into the air as her tail hit the wave.

The engines screamed as the pilot rammed on full power. She hurtled forward, charging the next wave and the port float hit it first, digging into the crest and pulling the bulk of the aircraft round in a wild circle. The port wing dug deep into the sea and the

Sunderland rose like a giant whale thrashing the surface. Her starboard wing lifted vertically into the sky as the whole aircraft cartwheeled, her engines howling out of control. A flicker of flame swept the wing and found the fuel tank, igniting the petrol inside and exploding into a ball of fire which engulfed the wing. For a fleeting second, the aircraft continued her cartwheel then levelled out on to the water amid a vast mountain of spray which doused the flames. She settled nose down with her tail jutting high into the air.

Inside the Sunderland the twelve-man crew had taken a fearful battering but all of them had survived. The skipper of the Sunderland had spotted the Whitley's dinghy floating some distance from Triggs' craft. His own dinghy was punctured and useless and their only hope was to reach the empty dinghy. One of his crew, a Sydney-born man called Watson, was a strong swimmer and volunteered to swim for the dinghy. He launched himself into the wild sea and fought his way through the waves until, in a state of complete exhaustion, he reached it and hauled himself aboard. Then began the herculean task of paddling the dinghy back to the Sunderland. He tried desperately, knowing that the lives of his crew depended upon his reaching the sinking aircraft but the effort was too much and he collapsed.

The sea poured into the Sunderland and she sank lower until at last she was gone, taking the remaining eleven men with her.

None of this was known to the men huddled in Triggs' dinghy. The Whitley dinghy which they could barely see in the distance had raised a flag and they assumed that the crew of the Sunderland had managed to get aboard her. It was not until later that they were to discover the full horror of what had happened.

Another night began, dogged by sea-sickness, biting winds and, worst of all, the possibility that they might sink at any moment. A hole had developed in the dinghy and a rubber stopper plugged it temporarily.

Because of the constant sea-sickness none of them had been able to eat. The result was that they grew even weaker, their chilled and numbed bodies limp and helpless. They shivered uncontrollably as the night dragged on.

At last dawn came. From time to time as the dinghy rose in the swell they caught fleeting glimpses of the other dinghy but it brought little consolation.

The sky brightened and the wind dropped but the sea continued its onslaught. In the course of the morning they saw several aircraft some distance away from them, clearly hunting for them and the crew of the Sunderland. The Very pistol would be of no use at that range so Triggs wisely decided to conserve his cartridges.

The aircraft continued to scout the area throughout the morning, then the search stopped. No more aircraft were seen until around 16.00 hours when a lone Beaufighter came into view. She fussed around some distance away gradually making her way closer to the dinghy. Triggs decided the time was right to fire a cartridge but the Beaufighter crew missed it. He fired another then another until he was pumping them into the sky sending up a blazing display of pyrotechnics. Then the Beaufighter turned in their direction. It looked as if they had been seen – but the Beaufighter never reached the dinghy. Instead she began circling about half a mile from them. She had found the other dinghy but she did not linger and set course for England.

An hour later two Whitley bombers droned towards them. One of them flew low and dropped another bag of emergency supplies then turned tail and headed for home while the other began signalling to the dinghy. A naval destroyer was on its way to pick them up. Roars of joy came from the bedraggled and soaked men in the dinghy but it was soon cut short. The Whitley's signal lamp flickered again. The destroyer had been recalled to base because of bad weather.

A moment later the throb of the Whitley's engines roared in a crescendo as it fought to gain height. The urgent tone suggested that there was trouble about. The men in the dinghy looked around and then they saw them; three German fighters hurtling across the sky in pursuit of the Whitley. The bomber only just reached the sanctuary of the clouds in time. With luck the Whitley would escape unmolested. There was, however, the very real possibility that Triggs' dinghy had been spotted by the fighter pilots. When they found the Whitley gone they might return to machinegun the occupants of the dinghy. It had happened before – or so rumour had it. As a precaution, the men in the dinghy took off their jackets and spread them over the dinghy, hiding the yellow rubber. It was then that an explosion followed by a towering black pall of smoke betrayed the fate of the Whitley. She had not had a chance. Triggs and his crew were horrified. Two aircraft had been lost in the attempt to rescue them. None of them spoke; they were too overcome with grief to express their emotions.

When the last light of day was fading events looked as if they might take a dramatic turn. One of them spotted a boat coming out of the gloom from the direction of the French coast. It was a French fishing boat and if it held its course it would pass within a short distance of them.

Even in their pitiful and depressed state they knew that they must not fall into the hands of the enemy. If the French trawler picked them up it could well mean a prisoner of war camp for the duration of the war. None of them wanted that.

The French boat continued on its course and the men in the dinghy crouched low to diminish their profile. It worked. The boat chugged past.

The night passed and the dawn brought with it a

white mist that clung to the sea and shrouded the dinghy. The dense fog was known to hug the Bay of Biscay for days on end. If the mist persisted, they reasoned, they had had it. Visibility was barely a mile during the best part of the day and they were just a tiny yellow speck in the grey sea.

Throughout the day they saw only one aircraft and that was German. Evidently the search for them had been called off until the weather improved. The ever-resourceful Badham busied himself fashioning a sea-anchor out of the materials they had at their disposal. To everyone's astonishment, it worked and it held the dinghy on course. But while this helped to give them a sense of usefulness, another menace loomed.

One of them spotted a black fin slicing through the water in their direction. There was no doubt about it, it was a shark. A determined shark could overturn the dinghy and make a hearty meal of its passengers. They prepared to fight it off. Triggs levelled the Very pistol, their only weapon. If the shark looked as if it was about to attack, a cartridge from the pistol might scare it off.

The creature swept around the dinghy, perhaps considering whether or not to attack. Triggs held his fire. These were nervous moments but at last the shark swam off. The airmen flopped back into the dinghy. Whatever danger there may have been, the incident did serve to break the monotony of an otherwise tedious day.

Night came once more, another night of bitter cold and perpetual motion. It was easy then, in the darkness, to give up hope, to let go and simply fade into unconsciousness and ultimate death. The following day was a carbon copy of the previous one. Again the mist hugged the sea and they saw no aircraft. Again the search had had to be postponed and they settled in for another night with growing despondency.

Both physical and mental exhaustion combined to produce weird hallucinations among the crew. Subjection to such conditions was known to result in odd behaviour.

Cartwright dozed fitfully as the hours passed. Then suddenly he saw something not far from the dinghy. He could not believe his eyes. There were two towering columns – the supports of a quay! He shouted to the others. They had drifted into a harbour. His companions shook themselves and looked around, straining their eyes to confirm Cartwright's revelation. They could see nothing.

'Try and get some sleep,' one of them said. 'You're seeing things.'

Cartwright looked again. The 'harbour' was gone. He had imagined it all. Annoyed with himself for submitting to the illusion, yet convinced that he had seen something, he tried to reason it out. Then he saw what had caused it. His tired eyes had mistaken the heads of two of his companions for the supports of the quay. In the darkness they had seemed distant and taller than they were. He cursed himself for being so stupid and tried to get some sleep.

But sleep eluded him and the others. The heavens opened and the rain poured down in a violent torrent. However, the rain proved refreshing and the weather changed. The wind altered direction, forcing the dinghy off its course towards England.

Next day the sun gave them fresh heart. Now the search would be resumed – but the morning passed without sight of searching aircraft or ships. Unknown to them there *were* aircraft looking for them but it was the early afternoon before they caught sight of one of them, a Beaufighter which darted across the sky on a course which would have missed them. Triggs fired the Very pistol, not really expecting the flare to be seen but the sharp-eyed crew of the Beaufighter saw it and changed course.

The fighter zoomed over them, waggling its wings. Then it flew off, radioing the dinghy's position to another Beaufighter over the horizon.

The thoughts of the men in the dinghy had never been far from the survivors of the Sunderland and when the other Beaufighter arrived she signalled them to make contact with the other dinghy and advised them that there was *one* wounded man on board.

For a moment Triggs and the others thought there must have been some sort of mistake. Surely there must be more than one man left out of that crew.

The other dinghy was almost a mile away from Triggs' craft. The sea was running against them but they knew they would have to make the effort to reach it. Badham took in the sea-anchor and they took turns at paddling. From time to time, with the waves rising several feet, they lost sight of the other dinghy and the pilot of the Beaufighter, sensing their difficulty, flew over the other craft to mark its position.

Then, as they narrowed the gap, two Hudson bombers appeared over the horizon. The bomb doors on one of them opened and three objects tumbled out. For a horrifying moment, they thought the Hudson had spotted a U-boat and had dropped depth charges. But when they did not explode, the men in the dinghy ventured a look. The Hudson had dropped another dinghy and two emergency supply packs which floated within easy distance of the dinghy. But it took all their strength to reach them, and then they found that the new dinghy was overturned. They stripped off their clothes, plunged into the icy cold sea, swam for the upturned dinghy, then towed it to their own. Righting the dinghy was beyond their strength and they decided to salvage what they could from it.

The aircraft still buzzed around above them but its fuel was running out. With a farewell swoop, they departed.

They were not alone for long. As soon as the British aircraft had left more aircraft appeared. They were four small hornet-like fighters bolting across the sky. As they shot closer there was no mistaking their identity; they were German FW 190 fighters.

The fighters were bearing down fast on the dinghy. Even now as they drew closer the German pilots might be getting ready to rake the dinghies with fire. Nearer and nearer they came, heading straight for Triggs' dinghy. He was tempted to order the crew to abandon the craft in a bid to escape the fusillade of fire that must come. In a moment the fighters were on them – then they flashed past and were gone. Not a shot was fired. In fact Triggs could have sworn he saw the pilots waving in greeting. The fighters soared skyward and disappeared into the misty sky. Relieved, they dug their paddles into the water and headed once more towards the other dinghy. The going was tough but slowly they were making headway.

It took them almost five hours to reach the Sunderland dinghy. There they saw one soaked and spent soul lying on the point of collapse in the well of the dinghy.

The lone Australian summoned his strength to show some spark of wit. His face was drawn and white with salt spray. He attempted a smile as they hauled the dinghy closer to their own and pulled him on board. He seemed in a worse state than they were and could hardly lift a limb. Finally he slumped into the well.

Willing hands stripped him of his clothes and he was given a good rubbing down to restore some life to his frozen body. Then they dressed him in a protective suit which had been dropped from one of the rescue aircraft. Triggs prepared a meagre but welcome meal for him then lit one of their precious cigarettes for him. His hope of survival was restored now that he had some company.

Watson had seen the flight of German fighters and it was he who suggested they might be lurking not far off. He guessed that they might be waiting in ambush for the search aircraft when they came looking for the survivors. His prediction was right. Shortly afterwards a Beaufighter came into view. It skipped across the sky in the direction of the dinghy. Triggs was sorely tempted to fire off the Very pistol to attract the crew's attention but he knew that if he did, the German fighters might pounce.

Instead Triggs let the Beaufighter fly on. And then, as if from nowhere the German fighters appeared, screeching out of the sky and down after the British plane. But the Beaufighter crew had seen them and scurried off at full throttle.

The German fighters broke off the chase and departed, doubtless to wait for further fodder for their guns. It came later when a Sunderland flying boat appeared and thundered overhead. Triggs, fearing that they might cause the loss of another flying boat, did not signal but let it go on its way. The German fighters did not appear and to the best of their knowledge, the flying boat was not attacked. But the dinghy had been spotted by her crew and when she returned to base that night their exact position was passed on to other rescue aircraft which would take off before dawn the following morning.

With a newcomer on board to liven up the conversation, the night passed more happily. For the first time since they had crashed they all managed to get a reasonable amount of sleep.

Hudsons and Beaufighters appeared shortly after dawn and circled over the dinghy. From one of them a lamp flashed and the crew in the dinghy read the message. Help would be along shortly.

Greatly elated, the men in the dinghy scanned the horizon for a sight of their rescuers. It was then that they spotted trouble; German fighters circling and buzzing around as if homing in on something in the sea. They strained their eyes to catch sight of the ship that was the focus of the Germans' attention but could not make it out. Then off to the north, some distance from the Germans, they saw a vessel ploughing through the waves. At first glance she looked like the illusive destroyer that had been promised them days earlier but as she drew nearer it became clear that it was not one but four motor launches. It would not be long now before they were safely aboard. But Triggs was worried about the German fighters which were gradually getting closer and it looked as if the British aircraft had not seen them. They would be mauled if the fighters jumped them.

Soon the first of the motor launches was alongside and Triggs yelled to the captain, warning him of the German fighters. In a moment the signal lamps were flashing to the British aircraft and the Hudsons climbed away to the safety of the clouds, leaving the Beaufighters to protect the rescue launches.

Then they saw the craft in which the Germans were taking such an interest. She was a German rescue launch sent out to snatch the aircrew from the dinghy before the British could get to them. Above her flew a posse of Arado fighters. Soaring across the sky from another direction came a flight of Focke Wulfe 190 fighters aiming to shoot down the Beaufighters but the British airmen saw them and turned to the attack. While a battle royal was fought out above them Triggs and the others were hauled aboard the rescue launch and shepherded below decks.

In the air, one of the 190s bolted skyward with a trail of smoke streaming out of her. The battle continued and some of the German fighters turned their attention to the motor launches as they raced at full speed for home. Machinegun and cannon fire spattered the sea. Triggs, peering out from a hatch, wanted a crack at the attackers and asked the captain if he and his men could man the guns.

'Help yourselves!' he said, amazed at the stamina of these men.

Triggs and his men manned the anti-aircraft gun, pumping shells into the sky at the Germans. But the British aircraft were winning the day in a furious dogfight. Then one of the Germans came into the sights of Triggs' anti-aircraft gun, just long enough for a burst of fire to hit it. Immediately the fighter began belching smoke and she turned to limp off for home. Moments later the bulk of the Germans fled. But, at a safe distance, the German launch and its umbrella of fighters lurked in the wings, waiting their chance. Only minutes later, a JU 88 dive bomber hurtled down out of the sky to bomb the launches but she did not get far. Before she could release her bomb, a Beaufighter lashed her with fire. She pulled crazily out of her dive and wavered drunkenly as she made for her base.

As a constant reminder that they had not been forgotten, a Condor four-engined bomber shadowed them from afar but he, like the German motor launch and her attendant Arados, had to give up as the tiny fleet of boats and Beaufighters neared home.

At last England came into sight and soon the survivors were enjoying a hot meal, followed by sleep and a protracted leave before returning to operational duties.

Triggs and his crew had been plucked from the sea to fight another day but the cost of their rescue had been high. They had spent a total of 124 hours in the sea and seventeen men had perished trying to save them. But their sacrifice had not been in vain. The story of the epic rescue gave confidence to other RAF aircrews. They knew that if they crashed into the sea no effort would be spared in rescuing them.

4

A Bird in the Hand

Squadron-Leader Cliff's Beaufort torpedo-bomber 'M Mother' lanced out across the North Sea from her base at Sumburgh in the Shetland Islands off the north coast of Scotland. It was late February 1942 and Cliff's aircraft, along with five others, was en route for the southwest coast of Norway, more precisely the stretch of sea between Stavanger and Kristiansand. Intelligence reports had indicated that a German capital ship was in the area and Cliff and his Beauforts were to find the German ship, radio back its position, then attack her. When the attack was over, they were to fly to Leuchars, an RAF base in Fife about eight miles south of Dundee on the river Tay.

M Mother's twin Taurus engines droned comfortably as Cliff nursed the Beaufort across a tempestuous sea below. Beneath him was one of the most notorious expanses of sea in the world; malicious and renowned for her eccentricity, respected by sailor and airman alike, the graveyard of many of them in the Second World War.

Over the previous few days Cliff had chased around Britain with 42 Squadron, moving from one RAF station to another following reports that the German capital ships *Scharnhorst*, *Gneisenau* and *Prinz Eugen*, based on the Atlantic coast of France, were planning a dash through the English Channel to join up with Germany's mightiest battleship *Tirpitz* at her anchorage in a Norwegian fjord. From there they would

threaten the Allied Atlantic convoys. Under cover of
bad weather and with an almost impenetrable umbrella of Luftwaffe fighters, the three ships made their
Channel dash, despite determined attacks by RAF and
Fleet Air Arm aircraft. Cliff was among those who
sought to stop the ships but without success. Now there
was uncertainty about their position. The RAF set out
to deal a fatal blow against the ships before they could
seek succour in the Norwegian fjords or some German
port. One of the ships had been reported steaming
towards the area Cliff and his aircraft were about to
search and it was with growing anticipation that M
Mother neared the Norwegian coast.

The other five aircraft flew on parallel courses farther
north, enabling them to cover the widest possible area
in their search. Cliff, with the longest flight of them all,
had left Sumburgh earlier than the others and was expected to return later than them.

In the belly of the Beaufort hung a slender cigar-
shaped torpedo, the weapon with which Cliff aimed to
put paid to the German ship. In the perspex nose of the
aircraft Flying Officer McDonald, the navigator,
busied himself with alterations in course that would
bring them into the Norwegian coast. Behind the
armour plating at the back of Cliff's seat was the radio
equipment manned by Sergeant Venn, while still farther back in the fuselage Pilot Officer Tessier kept an
eagle eye open for marauding German aircraft. He,
along with Venn, manned the two free Vickers machineguns which were located on either side of the aircraft. Four men, intent and concentrating. But there
were other crew members in the aircraft; two passengers who were to play a vital role in the events that
were to follow. They were two homing-pigeons who
went by the names of 'Winkie' and 'Stinkie'. They
stood, completely unimpressed by the whole affair, in
strong wicker baskets close by Venn's radio equipment.

Both Winkie and Stinkie were something of a last

resort in the event of the aircraft crashing into the sea. As often happened when an aircraft got into trouble and had to ditch, there was no time to send out a distress signal. Then the pigeons came in. The pigeons wore tiny containers on their legs and the ditched crew could write a note, put it in the container and send the pigeon off in the hope that it might reach home and give the rescuers their position. Winkie and Stinkie both came from the pigeon loft of James Ross, a well-known pigeon fancier and breeder who lived on a farm close to Broughty Ferry, near Dundee and not far from Leuchars. Cliff and his crew hoped that they would never need to put their homing abilities to the test.

As the Beaufort drew closer to the Norwegian coast it came within range of enemy fighters. The cloud was low, giving them good cover and the sea was clear, making the job of finding the ship that much easier. Soon the backdrop of Norwegian coastline came dimly, then more positively, into view ahead of Cliff. When he had reached a point some four miles off Norway he turned south to patrol a line down the coast. There was no sign of the German ship.

Kristiansand came into view with its lighthouse just off the point and still the sea was deserted. By now they would have been picked up on the German radar and it was dangerous to linger too long within striking range of the Luftwaffe's Norwegian airfields. German fighters might already be airborne and homing on them.

Cliff was far from satisfied when the time came for him to change course and head for Leuchars. The broad expanse of the Skagerrak did, he felt, hold promise. Perhaps the German ship was not as far north as RAF Intelligence reports had claimed. She might still be ploughing her way over the Skagerrak. The intuition of the hunter niggled at his mind. There was enough fuel left for a quick sweep over the Skagerrak. After all, he was there and it seemed senseless to waste the opportunity. Resolved now, he held a southerly course, heading across the sea towards Denmark. But the sea was empty. Satisfied that he had done his best, Cliff asked McDonald for a course to steer back to Leuchars.

It was a little after 16.00 hours when the Beaufort banked round and began its flight back across the North Sea. The remainder of the sortie would be the usual tedium. At last the crew of M Mother could un- wind, Cliff brought the aircraft to five hundred feet then set her on automatic pilot. From here until she closed the Scottish coast, she could fly herself with few adjust- ments, cruising at around 160 miles an hour. As they widened the gap between themselves and the menace of the Norwegian coast their tension eased. McDonald produced a piping hot flask of tea and passed a cup to Cliff. He sipped the hot brew gratefully and leant back in his seat.

Disaster struck like a thunderflash. An ear-splitting roar jarred everyone on board. The port engine erupted in flames; the Beaufort slewed crazily and nose-dived straight into the sea. It thudded into the water amid a vast mountain of spray. Cliff was thrown forward, jab- bing his right arm into the control panel.

The impact sliced the wings off the Beaufort and shattered the fuselage but miraculously none of the men in the crew was badly hurt. Water poured into the broken aircraft and its icy cold jarred Cliff back to sensibility. He gaped in disbelief out to the sea ahead of him. There was the aircraft's yellow rubber dinghy, already inflated with Venn and Tessier inside it. The whole horror had happened in less than a minute.

Cliff wrestled out of his seat and swam out of the sinking Beaufort. McDonald was already clear and making for the dinghy. Venn and Tessier helped both men aboard and they slumped on to the rubber bot- tom, still unable to believe what had happened.

For a time they all sat speechless, trying to gather their wits. It was incredible that only minutes before they had been cruising happily above the North Sea and now they were in it. Clearly, there had been something very wrong with the port engine but Cliff had had no prior warning that it was not running well.

They were one hundred and fifty miles from home, a minute dinghy in a wilderness of sea with the odds weighted heavily against them. Cliff took stock of the situation. Grim as it was, it could have been worse. At least they had all got out of the aircraft alive. Cliff had injured his right arm but not seriously.

Sergeant Venn had, with remarkable presence of mind, grabbed one of the pigeon baskets as he fought his way out of the aircraft. Furthermore, Venn had managed, in the space of less than thirty seconds between the explosion in the engine and hitting the water, to send out a distress signal and lock in the transmitting key on the wireless. But it was a chance in a million that anyone had got a fix from the signal. Their principal hope rested upon Venn's pigeon. There was little they could do to get home by themselves, although Cliff had a small pocket compass which would give them an idea of their progress – if any – across the North Sea with the drift of the sea.

If they were to survive at all, rescue would have to come soon. They had no food except for a bar of chocolate, some milk tablets, and chewing gum – and they had no fresh water.

To add to this, the weather very quickly got worse and the clouds gave forth snow. Combined with the freezing wind and their soaked clothes, this could soon bring them death by exposure. It was still light but darkness was only a short while away. There would be no rescue that night. But Cliff forbade pessimism and persuaded his crew to think only of survival. They had the pigeon Stinkie, and at least he gave them some cause for hope. Winkie must have perished in the crash.

They set about preparing Stinkie for his flight home. Between them they found a pencil and a small piece of paper. On this they wrote their approximate ditching position. Then this was rolled up and slipped into a tiny cartridge which in turn was put into the container on Stinkie's leg. Then came the launch. Stinkie was urged into the air but had barely flapped his wings when he alighted on the inflated ring of the dinghy and stood there, clearly unwilling to undertake any flight at all.

The business of persuading the pigeon to return home was one fraught with difficulties. The vision of a homing pigeon that did not want to go home had a somewhat comic aspect but it was lost upon a soaked and frozen crew tossing about the North Sea in a tiny dinghy. Cliff tried a bit more persuasion and the bird did lift into the air, but Stinkie performed a quick flip around the dinghy then landed again upon the inflated rim. These circuits and bumps continued for some time and the antics of the reluctant flier brought a brief moment of humour. But since their lives seemed to depend upon the pigeon, Stinkie had to be made to fly off. They shouted at the bird and scared it by furious gesticulations, almost ending up in the sea in their attempts to launch him.

At last, Stinkie submitted and set course for Scotland and his loft in Broughty Ferry. There was, however, one problem. Pigeons do not fly at night and although Cliff and his crew were not absolutely sure of this, they had to reckon that Stinkie would settle on the sea until dawn. It was almost dusk when the pigeon left so he would not get much flying done that night. They estimated that the flight would take almost four hours, based on a flying speed of around forty miles an hour.

Cliff made his crew start paddling the dinghy towards Britain, not in the belief that they could make it back under their own steam, but to keep them all occupied.

At Leuchars they had waited with growing anxiety. As the minutes passed after Cliff's expected time of arrival the anxious watchers grew more and more certain that M Mother was not coming back. Initially they had reasoned that Cliff might have extended his patrol, but even taking that into account when the time drew near 20.00 hours, they knew that he must have crashed. It was then that the alert was raised and a search mounted. A Catalina flying boat was sent out into the night in the hope that she might spot wreckage or better still the dinghy with survivors, if indeed there were any. The crew of the Catalina was faced with an enormous problem. They had to assume that Cliff had come to grief somewhere along the route he would have taken if he had headed directly back towards Leuchars from Kristiansand. The Catalina flew that route and, of course, missed the dinghy. But even if they had known Cliff's approximate position, it was extremely unlikely that they would have been spotted in the fading light.

The morning brought greater hope when a Hudson bomber left Leuchars on a similar mission of mercy but her sortie was in vain. She retraced the route the Catalina had flown but saw nothing.

James Ross visited his pigeon loft in Broughty Ferry with almost ritualistic regularity every morning and that morning in February 1942 was no exception. But on that particular day he found one of his pigeons in a sorry state. It was covered in oil, its feathers matted with the thick black substance. He examined the ring on its leg and found that the bird was indeed his. The ring bore the registration number 1038. He remembered immediately that this was one of the birds he had given to the RAF but when he opened the cartridge container on the bird's leg – it was empty.

James Ross could have left the matter at that. Without anything in the container, the bird might well have been of no use to anyone. It might simply have escaped and flown home. There was no apparent reason to treat its sudden reappearance as of any great significance. But James Ross's intuition told him that something was amiss. His long experience as a pigeon fancier told him that the bird had come quite a distance, possibly more than a hundred miles. If the bird had escaped from Leuchars, which was some ten miles from Broughty Ferry, it would not have been in the exhausted state it was. There was clearly more to this than met the eye. He resolved there and then to phone Leuchars.

Ross was put in immediate touch with the duty controller at Leuchars and when he told him that one of his birds, registration number 1038, had returned in a pathetic state the controller was overjoyed. He checked the numbers of Winkie and Stinkie and found that the bird was from Cliff's aircraft. But his moment of joy was instantly shattered when Ross told him that there was no message in the pigeon's container. Nevertheless, they now had a lead, however slight it might be. They knew – or suspected – that at least one of the crew had got out of the aircraft alive and had been able to launch the pigeon. But since there was no note giving the position of the crash, there was cause to believe that the man might be very seriously injured. This made finding the dinghy quickly all the more urgent.

By then Ross had had time to consider the condition of the bird more closely and deduce from from that its probable flight. The fact that it was covered with oil suggested that it might not have flown as far as he had first imagined. Bearing in mind that he had found it about an hour after dawn, it could not possibly have flown very far. His second estimate therefore was nearer to some fifty miles.

Vague as it was, even this information could be of inestimable value to the controller and the navigating officer who was called in to give his expert advice. If Ross's judgement were anything to go by it meant that Cliff had crashed in the sea within fifty miles of the coast in the area of the Firth of Tay.

The RAF men drew out the area in which the crash could have happened and search aircraft were quickly airborne and scouring the sea within a fifty-mile radius of Broughty Ferry. Hudsons and Beauforts carried out the search and overflew the sea for the next hour but found nothing. The result was hardly surprising for Cliff and his crew were a further hundred miles away, suffering the rigours of biting cold and nausea.

It seemed now that they were lost for ever. But the RAF at Leuchars did not give up. The navigation officer decided to probe Ross's considerable experience with pigeons a little further. It could not do any harm and he thought there might just be something he had overlooked.

He spoke to Ross again and found the pigeon fancier even more puzzled than ever. Ross had mulled the thing over in his mind and come to the conclusion that the bird would have found it very difficult to have flown at all, never mind the distances he had previously suggested. It was so thickly covered with oil that flight over a long distance would have been all but impossible. Ross told the navigation officer and then the question was posed that, since the bird must have flown at least some distance, it must have got the oil over its feathers from somewhere – but where? Ross suggested that it might have come from the crash but this was discounted as extremely unlikely. There were no large oil depots in the Broughty Ferry area. So how was it that the bird had got itself covered in oil?

The telephone line was silent for a few moments as the two men wracked their brains for a logical answer to the mystery. And then it came to the RAF man. The pigeon must have got the oil from a tanker. It seemed the only answer. The pigeon would not fly at night and when darkness came, it must have alighted on a passing oil tanker in the North Sea. Since it was on the tanker and would have remained there for the night, presumably it must have been a passenger throughout the night and travelled with the tanker. This theory held water only if there had been a tanker in the area the night before.

The navigation officer contacted shipping control at Rosyth on the River Forth near Edinburgh. He was told that there had in fact been a tanker sailing north throughout the previous night and its position at dawn that morning was almost directly opposite the Firth of Tay. It seemed too good to be true, but their thousand-to-one shot was paying off. Just as the controller and navigation officer were consulting the map to determine the approximate position of the tanker at dusk the previous evening, they got news that an army unit had picked up a faint distress signal at about 16.30 hours the previous evening. There was a possibility – a remote one – that it was a signal from Cliff's aircraft, but the army had been unable to get a positive fix.

If the distress call had in fact come from Cliff's aircraft it meant that the pigeon had less than an hour and a half flying time and could have covered no more than seventy miles. Knowing the position of the tanker at dusk, they were able to trace a line across the North Sea from that point for a distance of seventy miles and thereby arrive at a position where the aircraft might have crashed. It was a shot in the dark but a chance worth taking.

There was already a squadron of aircraft searching the North Sea for the crew, and a wireless message diverted them towards the area where the Beaufort was now thought to have gone down.

It was towards mid-day that Cliff and the others first saw the Hudson bomber hunting for them. Soon it was thundering overhead and dropped a bag of supplies which Cliff eagerly retrieved from the sea.

In Leuchars they heard that Cliff had been found and four air–sea rescue launches were dispatched from various ports to pick them up.

Almost an hour after the Hudson had departed another aircraft flew into sight. She was a Walrus sea plane. She sank from the sky and landed not far from the dinghy then taxied over. Soon they would be home.

The pilot of the Walrus popped his head out of the cockpit window and enquired of Cliff if his was the crew of a crashed Wellington. Cliff said they were not. With a muttered apology, the pilot revved up his engine and took off, leaving a totally bewildered Cliff and crew still in their dinghy.

A little after 14.00 hours they saw the first launch ploughing through the sea towards them. Soon they were on board and at 15.30 hours they were back on dry land, exhausted, frostbitten and tired. They owed their lives to a pigeon and they were naturally anxious to make their thanks both to the pigeon and to James Ross.

A meeting was arranged and they were asked why they had not put a message in the pigeon's container. Cliff emphatically claimed that they had put a message in the container and wondered why Stinkie had not had it when he reached the loft. It was then that James Ross confounded the enigma when he announced that the pigeon they held so gratefully in their hands was not Stinkie – but Winkie, the bird they had thought had perished in the crash. He must have escaped from the crash and made his way back to Broughty Ferry. As for Stinkie, he was never seen or heard of again. Winkie was awarded the Dickin Medal, the animal VC. He died some eleven years later, and was stuffed and put on exhibition in the museum at neighbouring Dundee where he can be seen to this day.

5

The Devil's Doctor

Felix Kersten's eyes scanned the grey portals of 8 Prinz Albrechtstrasse in Berlin. Outwardly, the building was much the same as any other in the wide thoroughfare. It was big, imposing, and with a somewhat forbidding frontage. Atop it fluttered the banner of Hitler's Third Reich, the black, red, and white swastika. But for one extra, that was where the similarity with its neighbours ended. Outside the gaunt building, flanking the big door, stood two sentries, proud, erect, and motionless, their eyes fixed and staring straight ahead. They might have been robots, puppet-like with sculptured, wooden expression, a matching pair clad in black uniforms, black jackboots and jet coat-scuttle helmets. Both were tall, of equal height, superb physique and clear blue eyes, their blond hair hidden beneath the helmets – perfect Aryans. They had to be. They were hand-picked members of the elite SS (*Schutzstaffel*), a corps of brutal thugs who, although war had not yet begun in March 1939, had already gained a terrible reputation for callous brutality towards the Jews in particular and any opponent of the Nazi regime in general. Number 8 Prinz Albrechtstrasse was the den from which their bestial crimes were directed. It was here that Heinrich Himmler, the Reichsführer SS, boss of the elite corps and the Secret State Police, the Gestapo (*Geheime Staats Polizei*), held court and planned the mass extermination of the Jews and other 'undesirables'. It was from here that the most heinous crime of modern times was planned under Himmler's direction.

Himmler's lair was a place to be avoided but it was to there that Dr Felix Kersten had been 'invited' by no less a personage than the Reichsführer himself. In Nazi Germany, an invitation such as this was not ignored.

Kersten had no idea why he had been summoned. By profession he was a manual therapist, specialising in the relief of pain by massage. He had built up a considerable reputation throughout Europe and had treated such dignitaries as the Crown Prince Hendrik, the husband of Queen Wilhelmina of the Netherlands. What then could the Reichsführer SS possibly want of him? True, he had treated Jews in the past. But was that a crime? Knowing little of the workings of the SS and Gestapo, he discarded that idea. Had he known better, he might have crossed the threshold with some trepidation, for association with Jews was sufficient for condemnation.

Kersten was a man of very considerable talent, a man with magic in his hands. Born in Estonia in 1898 he became a Finnish citizen after the First World War and travelled to Helsinki where he undertook a lengthy course in therapeutic massage. Helsinki was the acknowledged centre for the study of this form of treatment and it was while working at the hospital there that Kersten was nurtured by an eminent practitioner of manual therapy, a Dr Colander. He saw great potential in his pupil and took a special interest in him. Colander's faith in Kersten was fully realised and the young doctor emerged with a degree in manual therapy.

Kersten moved on to Berlin to broaden his experience. It was there that he met Dr Ko, an aged Chinese master of the art of massage. Ko had learned skills in Tibet where he had become a lama but he had known the art of massage since childhood. After twenty years of intensive study he had qualified as a doctor and practised both in Britain and Germany. Ko never prescribed medicines; he used only his skill in massage derived entirely from his studies in Tibet, and treated his patients exclusively with his hands.

Ko took a liking to Kersten and asked him to show him how far he had advanced in the application of his skill. Kersten obliged but Ko was not impressed. He told him in a paternal way that 'he knew nothing' and offered to tutor him. Kersten grabbed at the chance and for the next three years rarely left Ko's side. He learned the secrets of the master's technique and became highly skilled in its use. Ko never pretended that the use of therapeutic massage could cure everything but he showed Kersten how a staggering number of complaints could be relieved and even cured.

In 1925, Ko told Kersten that he could teach him no more and they parted company, Kersten to embark upon a mercurial career which brought him considerable wealth and social standing. Invited to Holland to treat the Crown Prince he liked the country so much that he set up home and a practice there. In addition, with his newly acquired wealth, he bought a magnificent estate outside Berlin where he lived for part of the time with his wife and children. There, he indulged himself in his one great love, eating. Life was good for Kersten. His practice was thriving; he had a loving wife and family and a beautiful retreat. He avoided politics: he was a doctor and as far as he was concerned, such things as the rise of the Nazi Party in Germany were outside his orbit.

Kersten, by now somewhat overweight, through indulgence in eating, passed through the doors of 8 Prinz Albrechtstrasse. A young lieutenant escorted him from the hallway to the very heart of the SS building.

'The Reichsführer will see you immediately, Herr Doktor.'

He opened a door and there, standing before a desk strewn with papers, was Himmler. The Reichsführer beckoned him to enter and Kersten did as he was bade. As the door closed gently behind him the doctor could see at once why he had been summoned. He had never met Himmler before but the expression on the Nazi's face was one he had seen often in the past. It was that of a man in great pain.

In the moments before Himmler spoke, Kersten studied that face. There was nothing about it to single Himmler out as anything special; no outstanding facial peculiarities. If anything, a rather ordinary countenance which might have been mistaken for that of a bank clerk; surprisingly nondescript considering his reputation. There was servility imprinted upon it. He had been denied at birth the striking facial characteristics of his fellow Nazi leaders. The face was fattish with a receding, weak chin. A thin-lipped mouth which until then had perpetually worn a flat smile cut across the upward slope of the chin. A plain nose held in place a pair of steel-rimmed glasses which enlarged two small almond-shaped eyes. It was here, in the eyes, that one could have discerned the character of the man. Within those eyes lay the sign, the steely gaze of the mass murderer; a man bent upon the extermination of an entire race. But it was a weak gaze that met Kersten. The iron determination was not there; the smile gone.

'Thank you for coming, Herr Doktor,' he said, as if Kersten had come of his own free will. 'Your reputation is considerable in Germany and indeed throughout Europe. I ...' he hesitated to admit that he was suffering but the driving pain forced him to admission. '... I have been suffering the most excruciating stomach pains. Everything has been tried. The best doctors in Germany ... but no one can relieve me. I can neither sit nor stand in comfort. You are my last resort. Do you think you can help me?'

Kersten cast a professional eye on the pathetic creature standing half-creased before him. Himmler was quite tall but with narrow shoulders which detracted from an otherwise fine frame.

'I shall have to examine you before I can determine

whether or not I can help you, Herr Reichsführer.'

'Yes, yes, of course,' Himmler said anxiously.

'Please take off your shirt and lie down on the couch,' Kersten requested, waving a hand towards a divan in the corner of the room.

Himmler hurriedly complied, then lay outstretched on the couch. The doctor drew up a chair and sat beside the Reichsführer, laying his hands upon the German's body. Himmler tried to relax as Kersten's large fingers traced a pattern across his flesh, stopping here and there to probe gently, the tips sinking into the fat. With each touch, Kersten felt for the symptoms that would disclose Himmler's trouble. He used no stethoscope nor any other instruments.

Kersten's fingers moved inquisitively down over Himmler's chest until they reached his stomach, then they prodded once more. The German's body jolted into rigidity as a jarring pain lanced through it. It was as if a red hot poker had been thrust the length of his body. He let out a cry. Kersten had found the weak spot. He prodded again. Another cry of pain. By now Himmler's body was drenched in sweat, the beads of salty perspiration rolling off it and soaking the couch on which he lay. His face was distorted out of all recognition. He moaned, begging the doctor to stop but Kersten was oblivious to his protestations. Himmler's stomach, the root of the problem, was on fire, engulfed in unbearable pain.

At last, mercifully, Kersten took his hands away. Himmler, drained of strength from the torture, slumped limp on the sofa, his face still contorted.

Kersten leant back in his chair, thoughtfully contemplating his patient. Then he sat upright.

'The trouble is certainly in your stomach. The nervous system is at fault. I can understand now why you are in such pain.'

'I have never known such agony,' Himmler admitted. 'The doctors have tried everything, including morphine, but nothing relieves it.' He looked up at the doctor, his small eyes pleading for help. Kersten was his last chance and he hardly dared ask the obvious question, but he summoned his nerve for the moment of truth.

'Can you help me, Herr Doktor?'

Kersten thought for a moment. Then gave his reply.

'That remains to be seen,' he said with a hint of doubt in his voice, 'but I shall try now.'

Kersten laid his hands on Himmler's abdomen once more.

'Relax as best you can,' he commanded firmly. 'This will hurt a great deal – but it is for the best.'

Himmler had only a fraction of a second to prepare himself before Kersten's hands plunged into his fleshy stomach. The beefy hands seemed to sink right into him then grasp his innards and knead the flesh with malicious force. He almost passed out.

In the minutes that followed, Kersten subjected the German to a vicious torture as he manipulated the flesh, twisting it one way, then the other. The exertion was such that both men were soaked in sweat. To Himmler the treatment seemed worse than the illness itself and went on without end, until finally Kersten dropped back into his chair.

'There. It is done,' he said, sighing with exhaustion. 'That is as much as I can do for you this time.'

For a clear minute, Himmler lay still, not daring to move, fearful of putting the treatment to the test. Then he slowly began to pull himself up from the couch. Before the doctor's treatment this move would have brought a flash of searing pain to his body. But now, miraculously, as he drew himself higher, there was no pain. No fire swept through him. He stood upright, still unable to believe that the pain had gone – but Kersten's massage had worked. It was unbelievable – but true.

'This must be a dream!' the Reichsführer exclaimed

as he ventured a few steps across the room, still feeling no pain. 'This is more than I dared hope for, Herr Doktor.'

Himmler clasped him by the hand and pumped it in gratitude.

'You have performed a miracle.'

'It is no miracle, Herr Reichsführer,' the doctor disclaimed modestly, 'only the result of my long training. I ...'

'But it is!' Himmler interrupted. 'And you must be rewarded. I shall arrange immediately that you are appointed to the rank of SS colonel. You will be my personal physician, at my side at all times. I have great work to do. The Führer has entrusted me – yes me, Heini Himmler – with the final solution to the Jewish problem. No greater honour has been bestowed upon anyone. So you will understand that nothing must be allowed to stand in my way. Nothing! Illness must not distract me from my course. That must be clear to you, Herr Doktor? Then you will accept my appointment?'

Kersten was confused. Despite his lack of interest in politics and the antics of the Nazi party, Kersten had heard talk of Hitler's racism from some of his Jewish patients, and he knew he was on dangerous ground. He had no intention of becoming involved in any way whatever with Himmler's SS. But by the same token he dared not offend a man as powerful as the Reichsführer whose pen had already consigned thousands to the horrors of the concentration camp. Kersten knew that he would have to handle Himmler with great care and he searched his brain for a diplomatic escape route from the offer of high appointment.

'I am greatly honoured, Herr Reichsführer,' Kersten began. 'But I must respectfully decline your most generous offer. As I am sure you are aware, I live in Holland where I have my family and many patients who are in constant need of my care. I have a duty to them and so I am unable to accept. However, I do visit

Berlin regularly and, should you have need of me, I shall be only too glad to help in any way I can.'

'Of course, I understand, Herr Doktor,' Himmler said seriously. 'I too have a duty and where duty lies one must obey.'

Kersten had pulled it off. Himmler summoned one of his lieutenants and made it clear that Dr Kersten was to be admitted to SS Headquarters without question at any time he wished. He was a personal friend of the Reichsführer and was to be treated as such.

With that the meeting was over but not before Himmler had extracted a promise from Kersten that he would return daily until he was due to leave Berlin a fortnight later.

Kersten had no alternative but to comply, and he dutifully presented himself at Prinz Albrechtstrasse every day, where the treatment was continued.

Felix Kersten was well aware of the suffering Himmler had undergone. He also knew from past experience the degree of influence he would gain over a patient. The escape from pain brought moments of deep calm when the patient's gratitude for the relief was so profound that he was inclined to reveal his innermost secrets. In these early days with Himmler, it became clear that he too would conform to this pattern. But unlike Kersten's other patients, Himmler took advantage of the pauses between bouts of massage to indulge in excited diatribes on the superiority of the German race and how the 'verminous Jews' would have to be purged from the face of the earth.

To Himmler, Hitler was a god whose word was sacrosanct. The utterances of the Führer, however fanatical or perverse, were to him Commandments to be obeyed without question. When he mentioned Hitler's name, and that was often, Himmler's face lit in adulation. Under the Führer's leadership Germany would dominate the world and rid it of its 'scum' – and that meant every Jew.

At no time did Kersten enter into the conversation with Himmler on the subject of the Jews. He vowed to keep the relationship strictly on a doctor/patient basis but when, during a brief pause in the massage, Himmler revealed that Germany would soon be at war, Kersten could contain himself no longer.

'War? But why?' Kersten asked in stark amazement.

'It is the Führer's wish,' Himmler replied, as if that were all the explanation that was required. But he continued when he saw that Kersten was not convinced. 'It is the Führer's belief that the Reich will gain strength from it. War brings out the best in man. It is for the good of the greater Reich. *There must be war!*'

Kersten was incredulous. If what Himmler said were true then Europe would become a bloody battleground simply to satisfy the crazy notions of a power-mad maniac. The prospect was too awful to contemplate.

'Europe is wasted and corrupted by Jews,' Himmler went on. 'It is the Führer's mission in life to purify the system so that there will emerge a race worthy of his leadership – a new, greater Reich with Germany at its centre. The human race will one day revere the Führer as its saviour.'

Since first being summoned to Himmler, Kersten had acquired a new awareness of the dreadful persecutions that were going on around him. He saw for himself Himmler's thugs making their arrests, dragging off Jews and anti-Nazis to incarceration and ultimate death in the concentration camps. He saw the Jewish shops closed and boarded with anti-semitic slogans scrawled upon them. In the German newspapers he read condemnatory editorials from the pen of Dr Josef Goebbels, Hitler's Propaganda Minister, whose scathing prose did much to fan the flame of anti-semitism in the hearts of the Germans. The Nazi terror was complete. The horrifying spectre of persecution, suspicion, fear and violence haunted Germany – and it frightened the Finnish doctor.

Kersten was faced with a dreadful dilemma. He had, through no fault of his own, become inextricably embroiled. By treating Himmler and relieving him of his pain, he was directly enabling him to prosecute his heinous crimes. Himmler was almost totally dependent upon Kersten's ministrations to get him through his long working days. But at last a time arrived when he seemed well and Kersten returned to Holland and his other patients. But the doctor was still a very worried man. He knew that Himmler's pain would return and the call would inevitably come for him to go back to Berlin to treat him.

Kersten searched his brain for a way out. He could flee the country with his wife and family but in doing so he would be deserting the many other patients who depended upon him. This thought was considered and discounted. He could refuse to treat the Reichsführer but he had seen and heard only recently the fate that befell those who did not comply with the wishes of the Nazis. The Nazi tentacles reached far and he feared for the safety of his family if he took such a course.

As he had predicted, he was urgently summoned to Himmler's headquarters when he visited Berlin three months after his first session with the Reichsführer. Himmler was in immense pain but Kersten's hands very quickly brought him relief. As the German lay upon the couch, tranquillised by Kersten's massage, he confided in his doctor once more. The monologue turned to war. Himmler's assurance that the war would be short did nothing to allay Kersten's dread of the consequences for Europe. Until then Kersten had allowed Himmler uninterrupted speech, but now, with the certainty that the Reichsführer was dependent upon him, he ventured a few critical interjections. While treading warily in what he said, he was determined to ensure that Himmler did not construe his silence as condoning the Nazi crimes.

But Kersten's criticisms were wasted. To any logical

question he put forward by way of argument Himmler merely replied with a smile, 'It is the Führer's wish.'

War came in September 1939 when the might of Nazi Germany struck at Poland. Now, more than ever, Himmler was pressed to the limit. He worked from early morning into the night, organising the fate of three million newly-acquired Polish Jews. The added burden brought another bout of pain at a time, from Himmler's point of view, that he could least afford to be incapacitated. He called in Kersten to alleviate the worst pain he had ever suffered. The taxing pace of his work had almost crippled him and now, again, he was virtually at Kersten's mercy. The doctor, troubled by the events that were overtaking Europe, remained almost mute throughout the sessions of massage. After the treatment, Himmler was his old self again. His piercing eyes shone in crazed fanaticism as he preached the superiority of the Nazi ideals. But Kersten was distracted. There seemed to be no one to whom he could turn to for advice. He was alone with an incredible burden upon his shoulders. He had long thought of his adopted country, Finland. Despite the fact that he had rarely been there since taking up residence in Holland and Germany, he was still a Finnish citizen and an officer in the reserve army. There was the Finnish embassy in Berlin and he went there, hoping that someone might be able to advise him.

Kersten was granted an audience with a group of diplomats. He told them the whole story, of Himmler's illness, his treatment, and the confidences of the Reichsführer. The diplomats were awestruck at Kersten's revelations. He had the trust and confidence of the most feared man in Europe, and Himmler, in his moments of tranquillity immediately following treatment, was given to indiscretion. Kersten was privy to some of the Nazi State's most closely guarded secrets. Now Kersten wanted to know what he should do. Should he continue treating Himmler? That was the burning question.

In the minds of the diplomats there was absolutely no doubt. Not only should Kersten treat Himmler – he *must* treat him and keep in touch with the embassy to pass on any information which might be of use to the Finns. Kersten had unwittingly become a spy. But however distasteful the prospect, he did now at least have some official blessing.

Hitler's armies were ravaging Europe. Holland fell to the Wehrmacht and the Dutch Nazis emerged in strength, bent upon routing all opposition to them by the same techniques of intimidation and elimination employed by their German counterparts. Anyone who was not sympathetic to them or could not be bent into supporting the new regime was marked down for 'attention'. Kersten was one of them. He had treated the Crown Prince and in the eyes of the Dutch Nazis that was sufficient to mark him as 'undesirable'.

It seemed as if fate were closing in for the kill, and there was no escape from his predicament. Estonia, the country of his birth, had been annexed by Russia, against whom Kersten had fought in 1919. The twenty-one-year gap did not pardon his 'crime' and he was regarded by the new masters in Estonia as a traitor. The penalty was death, so that he faced liquidation in two countries. Even Finland, his adopted country, had closed her doors to him since he was under orders to continue Himmler's treatment. In Germany he was regarded with suspicion. His closeness to the Reichsführer SS nurtured jealousy among other prominent Nazis, notably the notorious Gestapo boss Reinhardt Heydrich who, although answerable to Himmler, had his sights set on greater power. He saw Kersten as a dangerous intruder. He therefore took steps to restrict Kersten's freedom of movement within Germany, particularly when the Wehrmacht thrust west into Holland. Kersten felt like a prisoner, penned into claustrophobic subservience to Himmler. Although the Reichsführer SS continued to treat him as a friend,

his attitude showed a marked change. Prior to the outbreak of war, Kersten's visits to Himmler had been by
invitation, but now he was ordered to attend. In May
1940 he was directed to accompany the Reichsführer
in his special train to the Western Front where the
German army was forging through France. Himmler's
elaborately-equipped personal train was almost in the
van of the thrust and from it he directed the operation
of the units under his control. He treated his mission of
Nazification as of the utmost urgency. Although he
had no record of military service he longed to command an army, and he revelled in his involvement at
the front. But the direction of his duties demanded that
he should be fit, and this was where Kersten came in.
Himmler did not care a fig for Kersten's other patients.
The disciple of death believed his mission to be above
all others. Nothing must be allowed to impede him.

Between Himmler's increasingly frequent daily sessions of treatment Kersten witnessed the horrors of war.
To escape this, he retreated to Himmler's private
mobile library where he found to his astonishment row
upon row of books on the subject of religion. Knowing
Himmler's obsession with Nazism and fanatical opposition to Christianity, he asked him why his library
was very largely devoted to volumes on the world's
religions. Himmler's answer was perhaps predictable.
He was engaged on writing a bible for the Nazi faith.
A time would come, he assured Kersten, when
Christianity would be replaced by a new religion in
which Hitler was recognised as the Saviour and to
whom all prayers would be said. God would be
'retained' but the emphasis would be directly upon the
Führer. The form of worship would be modelled upon
certain facets drawn from a variety of existing religions,
hence his intensive study of theology.

This horrifying prospect left a deep impression upon
Kersten. Nazification was to be all-embracing; no
vestige of life was to be left untouched by it.

Kersten was spent both mentally and physically and he found his old taste for good food gone. He was all too conscious of the animosity felt towards him by Himmler's entourage of SS men. They wallowed in the successes of their army and in drunken revelry celebrated the victories scored by the Wehrmacht. Their vulgar and crude manners disgusted the doctor to such an extent that he could no longer eat at their table. He was desolate. But he discovered an ally in the most unlikely place . . .

Himmler had a private secretary, Rudolf Brandt, who was the Reichsführer's constant companion. It was Himmler who made the initial introduction. Kersten already knew Brandt from his visits to Prinz Albrechtstrasse, but the slight, bespectacled and studious secretary developed a severe stomach complaint and Himmler asked Kersten to treat him. The doctor naturally assumed that the Reichsführer's secretary would be a diehard Nazi and he approached the treatment with the same sense of distaste he had for his boss. But the doctor was wrong. He began Brandt's treatment and as the days passed dicovered that the secretary was the very antithesis of his Nazi boss. It transpired that he, like Kersten, was an unwilling recruit. A doctor of law, he had been drafted into Himmler's employ. As First Clerk to the State before the outbreak of war he was a natural choice for the task. Refusal of the appointment would have cast suspicion on him and brought the inevitable consequences. He was directed into the SS and applied the same diligence to the job that had won him high office in civilian life. Part of Brandt's function as Himmler's private secretary was to process the directives issued by the Reichsführer. These included orders for the extermination of the Jews. A bond of friendship grew between the two men; one that was to have a considerable effect upon Himmler's plans to wipe out the Jews.

The campaign in the west ended when France

capitulated. Kersten returned to Holland. The pace of work was exhausting, but at least it took his thoughts away from his obligation to Himmler. Occasionally he found time for a quiet weekend with his wife and family at his country estate outside Berlin.

Kersten's period of respite was brought to an abrupt end by an urgent demand for his attendance at Prinz Albrechtstrasse. He dashed there and found Himmler writhing in agony. He quickly got to work on him and soon the pain was relieved. Himmler lay on the couch, relaxed and oozing gratitude to Kersten.

'My dear friend. How can I repay you for what you have done for me? You have given me life and yet I have paid you nothing.'

Kersten had been careful not to accept payment since this would have put him on the SS payroll and made him little better than those he despised most. But even more than that, although it mattered not to Kersten, he knew that Himmler could not afford to pay him his large fees. Despite his exalted rank, the Reichsführer lived on a mere pittance compared with that of the others in the Nazi hierarchy who plundered the conquered countries of their treasures and dipped deep into the Party funds. Himmler had family responsibilities. He had a wife and child to support as well as a mistress and two illegitimate children.

Kersten explained why he was not charging fees by saying that he charged only for the completed cure – and Himmler was by no means cured. But this was not enough for the Reichsführer.

'I cannot allow you to remain unpaid for the treatment you give me,' he insisted. 'You must understand that it is not for me alone but for the Reich. I have been charged with an awesome task and it is only with your help that I can hope to complete it. I owe you so much.'

'You owe me nothing, Herr Reichsführer,' Kersten assured him.

'But I must pay you. Name your price.'

Kersten was not interested in money but he was determined to exact payment from Himmler and now was his chance. He drew a sheet of paper from his briefcase and presented it to Himmler.

'There,' he said with some trepidation, 'that is my bill. It is within your power to free that man. If you do, my fee will be settled in full.'

Himmler examined the paper. It was in the form of a memorandum and referred to a foreman who was in the employ of a wealthy friend, a patient of Kersten's. The wretched man had been thrown into a concentration camp simply because he was a member of the Social Democratic Party. In the eyes of humanity he had committed no crime. Kersten's friend had begged him to use his influence to have the man released. The doctor had explained that he had no influence over Himmler but he had agreed to try. The Reichsführer merely glanced at the paper then summoned Brandt to his room. The secretary entered.

'Brandt. See that this man is released at once,' he ordered, handing him the paper.

Kersten had succeeded. He now knew the extent of Himmler's gratitude and saw the way that he could use it. At last he had found a glimmer of light in an otherwise black void.

However, only days after Kersten had completed that session of treatment, Himmler summoned him to Prinz Albrechtstrasse. His face was grim when the doctor entered.

'I have been receiving some disturbing reports from my Gestapo agents in Holland,' he began. 'They tell me that you have, against my express wishes, kept on your flat there. Worse still, your circle of friends includes some undesirables. I must warn you that your continued stay in The Hague can only cast the gravest suspicion upon you. You have invited the attention of the Gestapo and of the Dutch Nazi Party. I can tell you, Herr Doktor, that they are fishing for evidence against you and if they get it there will be nothing I can do to prevent them taking the appropriate action.'

Kersten was stunned. It was true that among his acquaintances in The Hague there were many who were opposed to the new regime, but to discover that his association with them placed him in a dangerous position came as a shock. Evidently the Nazis were determined to get him. But he had not bargained for what was coming next. Himmler's expression changed to one of menace.

'I value you very highly, Kersten, but you must conform to the New Order. There can be no exceptions. I shall give you ten days to dispose of your house in The Hague. If you fail to comply with that order then I can no longer be held responsible for your fate. Furthermore, you must report to Gestapo Headquarters every day in The Hague. I would advise you to do as I suggest.'

The interview was over. The doctor returned to Holland to put his affairs in order. His arrival there brought yet another shock. There had been a dramatic upsurge in Gestapo activity. Every night, they would swoop on another unsuspecting citizen and subject him to brutal interrogation, torture, and humiliation. Invariably his family would suffer too. Deportation might and very often did follow where the unfortunate was taken to a German concentration camp, never to be seen or heard of again. An air of fear and distrust prevailed in the Netherlands. Kersten was infuriated because it seemed he could do nothing to fight this terror. But there came a situation which demanded bold action – and he took it.

A friend of his, who went by the name of Bignell, was arrested in one of the Gestapo's night swoops and dragged off to their headquarters. The doctor discovered this only when he went to visit Bignell and found the house swarming with Gestapo. When he tried to enter, his way was barred by one of the Gestapo thugs clad in the uniform of his calling, a large-brimmed hat pulled down over his eyes and a leather coat belted at the waist.

'What's going on? I want to see my friend Bignell,' Kersten demanded.

'Your friend, eh? So Bignell is a friend of yours, is he? You are not very particular about the friends you have, are you? Bignell is a traitor. Perhaps you are a traitor too, eh?'

Kersten could contain his fury no longer.

'Don't be impertinent!' he barked, taking the Gestapo man by surprise.

'Then if you are not a traitor, what – or rather who – are you?'

'I am Dr Felix Kersten and I demand to know what all this is about.'

The agent's eyes lit at the name. 'Kersten, eh? I have heard of you. So you are a friend of the traitor Bignell.'

'He's no traitor. I have never heard anything so preposterous in my life. Herr Bignell is one of Europe's most highly respected art dealers.' Kersten had bought several old masters from him. 'He's an old man. What possible interest could a man like that be to you?'

'That is a matter for the Gestapo – and no business of yours. Now get out of here – or you will be joining your friend.'

Kersten, red-faced and angry, cast caution aside and wagged a finger in the Gestapo man's face with a warning.

'You will hear more of this – you mark my words!' Kersten blurted, and then stormed off to Gestapo head-quarters.

Kersten, being the man he was, did not report to a petty official as others did but to the Gestapo chief in person, Walther Rauter, one of Himmler's lackeys, who viewed Kersten with contempt and was a prime mover in the witch-hunt against him.

After officially reporting to Rauter in accordance with Himmler's orders, he set about broaching the subject of his friend Bignell with uncommon vehemence. Rauter was momentarily taken aback.

'I warn you not to attempt to meddle in Gestapo business, Kersten,' Rauter boomed angrily.

'I am not meddling!' Kersten retorted. 'A friend of mine has been wrongfully arrested and I want him freed immediately.'

Rauter rose from his seat, crimson with anger.

'Freed!' he screamed. 'You have the gall to come here and demand the freedom of a traitor – a spy in the pay of the British. Who do you think you are, Kersten?'

'I can vouch for his innocence,' he parried with equal force.

'Kersten, listen to me – and mark my words closely. You have to report to me daily because you are under suspicion. Should I take notice of what you say – you who might well be occupying a cell along with your friend?'

By now Rauter was leaning menacingly across his desk. Beads of sweat rolled down his forehead and white froth issued from his mouth. Kersten stared at him. He knew that already he was in deep – deeper than was safe. There was no back-pedalling now.

'Very well,' Kersten said, composing himself. 'Since you choose to take no heed of what I say, perhaps you will listen to the Reichsführer SS. Pick up your telephone and get me Himmler.'

Kersten was no longer gambling with his friend's life. It was now his own. He would speak to Himmler – and if that did not work, he knew that Rauter would crush him.

'Himmler?' he blurted. 'You want me to telephone *Himmler* and ask if he will speak to *you*? Do you realise that even *I* cannot do that without going through my superior, Heydrich? It is impossible. No, I can't do it!'

'I promise you that if you do not, you will answer to

the Reichsführer,' Kersten warned. Now Rauter was on the defensive; he paused in indecision. Perhaps Kersten had more influence than he realised. He could lose nothing by trying.

'Very well, Kersten, but I warn you now, if you are fooling me, I promise you that I will take great pleasure in seeing you squirm for mercy when I get to work on you.'

Rauter picked up the receiver. A moment later it clicked and he spoke.

'Put a call through to SS Headquarters, Berlin. Dr Felix Kersten wishes to speak to Reichsführer SS Himmler.'

Rauter replaced the receiver.

'It is done,' he said. 'Now we shall see.'

Kersten felt uneasy. Perhaps he had gone too far. If Himmler was in the same mood as he was when he last saw him, then all was lost.

Neither man in the room spoke as the minutes slowly passed. Finally the phone jangled into life. Kersten almost jumped. Rauter answered it, his eyes creased in mockery. A voice spoke at the other end of the line and instantly Rauter's expression changed to one of incredulity. Ashen white, he sat bolt upright.

'Herr Reichsführer!' he stuttered, unable to believe it was Himmler. He passed the receiver over to Kersten. 'It is the Reichsführer – for you. He will speak to you.' Rauter's hand shook as Kersten took the receiver from him. Kersten, himself nervous at the reception his call would get, forced himself to speak.

'Herr Reichsführer, it is Kersten . . .' he began, but got no further.

'My dear Kersten. I have been trying to contact you. I need you desperately. I am in great pain.' The voice was weak and betrayed the agony Himmler was clearly suffering. Kersten could have cheered. He had him! Himmler's complaint could not have returned at a more fortuitous moment.

'Herr Reichsführer, it is I who am in need of your help . . .'

Himmler interrupted him impatiently. 'My body is racked by pain and I am unable to work. You must come to Berlin immediately.'

Kersten ignored the plea and pressed on with his own.

'A friend of mine has been unjustly arrested by your Gestapo. They insist that he is a spy. I know that he is no such thing. He is an old and trusted friend who means no harm to the Reich.'

Kersten was not finished but Himmler interjected in desperate agitation.

'What is the life of some Dutch nonentity alongside mine, Kersten? The urgency of my task is of paramount importance. I need you here – now!'

Kersten resolutely pressed forward with his point.

'With respect, Herr Reichsführer, my coming to Berlin would be a waste of time. My technique requires of me mental tranquillity. Without it my hands are powerless to heal. I cannot concentrate upon my work when the life of my friend is threatened. I ask only one thing – release him.'

There was a moment's pause, then Himmler demanded to speak to Rauter. Kersten passed the receiver to the mute Gestapo boss. Rauter spoke only once before returning the receiver to Kersten.

'Immediately, Herr Reichsführer.'

'Bignell will be released at once, Kersten,' Himmler informed him. '*Now* will you come to Berlin?'

'I shall be on the next train,' Kersten assured him, then hung up.

Rauter sheepishly showed Kersten to the door and bid him good day. It would be safe to say that neither man found it easy to believe what had happened in the last few minutes.

Outside, Kersten was still dazed. He had put his head in the lion's mouth and retrieved it unmolested.

To have had one man released was a feat of special good fortune but now he had succeeded in rescuing a suspected traitor who, for all he knew, might well be guilty. The influence he had over Himmler made him quake at the prospect. If he could pull off such an achievement then what other 'miracles' could he perform?

Kersten made his way to Berlin and Himmler. After treating the Reichsführer he saw Rudolf Brandt and told him of what had happened in Holland. Brandt was as stunned as Kersten had been but both men realised the possibilities Himmler's illness and Kersten's skill had. If Kersten could save two men then why not more? Brandt assured him of his co-operation.

'But we must be very careful, my friend. The slightest leak and we are both doomed. If the Gestapo finds out what we are up to, they will be merciless.'

'I know,' Kersten said gravely. 'I do not worry for myself but there is no point in acting rashly. If we are uncovered then many people will lose their lives as a result.'

The two conspirators talked at length about the dangers they would face. Not the least of them was the flood of letters addressed to Kersten from Holland. These were pleas for his intervention in the deportation of men, women and children from Holland to the death camps of Germany. The worry was that the letters might be intercepted by the Gestapo. But Kersten invented a novel and daring piece of deception by having them addressed to him via Brandt at SS Headquarters. He explained to Himmler that the letters were from a 'mistress' in Holland and that his affair with her was of the utmost secrecy. If his wife were to find out, it would ruin him. The ruse to foil his wife appealed to Himmler. With a pat on the back for Kersten and the assurance that he would not betray his little secret, he gave him his blessing. Himmler had played straight into Kersten's hands!

From then on Kersten got a steady flow of letters
from his 'mistresses'. In each of them was a request for
his intervention and, choosing his moments with great
care, he persuaded Himmler to release or pardon a
growing number of people. In Holland the Gestapo
from time to time received orders from Himmler to
release a prisoner for no apparent reason. The evidence
amassed against these individuals was often irrefut-
able but the release orders came direct from the
Reichsführer SS himself and were not to be questioned.
But as the months passed and more and more unfortun-
ates were freed, the very total of these orders was such
that it was brought to the attention of Reinhardt
Heydrich, who master-minded the operation of the
Gestapo. Kersten, although unaware of this, had
known all along that the day would inevitably come
when his subterfuge would be brought to light. The
important thing in his mind was to delay that day for as
long as possible so that more Dutchmen might be freed.

In times of good health Himmler was unapproach-
able, resolute in his determination to rid Europe of
every Jew. Kersten knew that any plea for clemency
then was wasted. But the Reichsführer's illness continued to return at intervals and it was then that
Kersten pounced. With each Dutchman who found
freedom, Kersten walked farther down the path of
certain discovery. And then, in January 1941, it
came . . .

Kersten was staying at a flat he had bought in Berlin
when the dread knock came at his door early one morning. Only half awake he rose from bed, annoyed at the
continuous and impatient pounding on his door.

The doctor opened the front door and there, framed
in the doorway, stood two Gestapo agents. One of them
perfunctorily produced a badge from his pocket, waved
it in Kersten's face, and re-pocketed it.

'Gestapo,' he announced, and took a step into the
hallway, forcing Kersten out of his path.

'You had better come in then,' Kersten remarked sarcastically.

In the lounge Kersten sat in an easy chair, wrapped in his dressing-gown. The two Gestapo officers refused his invitation to sit.

'What do you want with me?' Kersten asked with mock innocence, his mind abuzz with all the possibilities. He feared the worst but he composed himself.

The taller of the two men spoke.

'It is the question of your dealings with the Jews, Herr Doktor.'

Kersten's heart missed a beat. He had been discovered.

'The Jews?' he quizzed, playing for time.

'Yes. It has been brought to our notice that you have been treating Jewish patients.'

'Of course I treat Jewish patients. I am a doctor. It is my duty to treat any patient who needs my help, irrespective of his colour or creed.'

'That is not quite so. As a German, you are forbidden to minister to the Jews.'

'As a German I might be,' Kersten admitted. 'But I am not a German. You see, I am a Finnish citizen and therefore not subject to your laws.'

'Finnish?' the German asked. 'But you are German.'

'I can assure you, I am no such thing. If you will wait just a moment I can prove it.'

Kersten left the room and returned a minute or so later with his passport which he handed to the Germans who had been so insistent about his nationality.

'Well, Herr Doktor, it appears that we have been mistaken. I must apologise for the intrusion.'

'Now that you know, I can be assured of a full night's sleep in the future,' Kersten said boldly.

With that the two Gestapo men left but Kersten felt no sense of relief. He could not escape the thought that the Gestapo had not come for the purpose they stated. After all, it was certain that they had a file on him and would know that he was a Finn. Why then should they bother to come to his house to get information they already had? Sleep was pointless now, so Kersten made a pot of coffee and sat in the lounge, contemplating the events of that morning. The result of his deliberations was the conclusion that the Gestapo were on to him; that perhaps they had some tit-bit of information that gave rise to suspicion but not yet enough to arrest him. They would, he knew, not take a chance on arresting him on flimsy evidence because of his friendship with Himmler. It was clear that they were on to something and just biding their time until he made a slip. He determined there and then to be more cautious. But first he had a card to play that might get the Gestapo off his back for a while at least.

Not long after his encounter with the Gestapo, he had to call on Himmler to administer more treatment. When the session was drawing to a close, he mentioned to the Reichsführer that he had had visitors. Himmler went white with anger, grabbed his telephone, rang a number, and in a rage barked at the person at the other end.

'No one – repeat no one – is to interfere with Doktor Kersten.'

Kersten had scored another point with Himmler but already he had learned to be wary of the Gestapo. Himmler's warning could only serve to intensify the Gestapo's determination to pin something on him. It was evident that Reinhardt Heydrich had a hand in the persecution and was not likely to be put off by Himmler's warning. He had the cunning of a fox and was infinitely more devious than Himmler. Kersten knew he could expect more trouble from that quarter – and it came, but in an unusual way . . .

Kersten and Heydrich met 'by chance' one day towards the end of February 1941, just as Kersten was leaving Himmler's office. It occurred to him later that the chance meeting might have been a carefully planned encounter. Heydrich greeted Kersten with false cordiality.

'Ah, Herr Doktor,' he said. 'This is indeed fortuitous. I have been meaning to get in touch with you.'

'Well, now you have me,' Kersten observed. 'What is it I can do for you?'

'Well —' Heydrich searched for words, 'I would rather like to have a talk with you. I have a matter I should like to discuss. Perhaps we could arrange an early meeting?' Heydrich was a tall, erect and imposing figure resplendent in his black SS uniform and Kersten could almost sense the air of menace about him.

'Yes, I am sure that can be arranged. I am free tonight if that is convenient.'

Heydrich agreed, and they arranged to meet at the Gestapo offices that very evening.

Kersten arrived promptly at the arranged time and found Heydrich waiting for him in his office. But now there was no attempt at mock civility. Heydrich greeted him with a curt, 'Sit down, Herr Doktor.'

Kersten sat with hands clasped on his lap, displaying a relaxed countenance while Heydrich looked down at the papers on his desk, gathering his thoughts before beginning the monologue.

'Herr Doktor, there are those within the frontiers of the Reich who are opposed to the regime and would go to considerable lengths to see the downfall of the Third Reich. They conspire, sometimes alone and occasionally in groups to perpetrate acts of sedition. They attempt to interfere with our resettlement programme for the Jews.'

The 'resettlement programme' was the name given by the Nazis to the mass extermination of the Jews, and Kersten knew it. He was aware that this prologue was by way of a lure to catch him off his guard. But Kersten was more than a match for the wily Heydrich. He merely sat mute, neither agreeing nor disagreeing with what the Gestapo boss had to say. Heydrich searched the doctor's face for some hint that he had touched a nerve, but the face was impassive and neutral in expression.

'We know,' Heydrich went on, 'that you keep in touch with your friends in Holland and Finland and that from time to time you receive requests to intervene on their behalf when there are cases of resettlement.'

Kersten's face remained blank, showing nothing of the shock he felt at this revelation. He waited expectantly for what was coming next. But Heydrich's next statement came as a complete surprise.

'I should like to help you, Herr Doktor. Naturally it must be difficult for you to decide which of these people are genuine and which are simply using you. As you know, the Gestapo has at its disposal details of all the persons who make these pleas to you. I would be prepared to assist you in making up your mind about these individuals. All you need to do is give me their names and we can carry out the investigations for you.'

Although Kersten showed no sign of it, he was stunned at the offer. He had expected Heydrich to condemn him and possibly have him arrested, but this was too much. It was obvious that Heydrich naively believed Kersten would both incriminate himself and his friends who asked for help by giving him their names and address. But Kersten did not take the bait.

'Well, what do you think of my offer?' Heydrich asked.

'I am conscious of your concern and I am sure that the Reichsführer will be pleased.' With that, Kersten left, secure in the knowledge that it would now be only a matter of time before his neck was in Heydrich's noose. He went directly to see Brandt and told him of his interview with Heydrich. Brandt turned pale.

'Heydrich is playing cat-and-mouse with you, my friend,' he warned. 'That meeting was by way of a warning – a threat of what is to come. He simply wanted to show you that he knew what was going on. Take my advice. Lie low for a while. Make no more requests for leniency for some time. You must not give Heydrich any more ammunition against you. If Heydrich thinks you've taken the warning seriously perhaps he will leave you alone and when the time is right you can return to your good work.'

'Yes, Brandt, you're of course right, although I hate to think of these people going to their deaths when I could do something to help.'

'You must close your mind to it, Herr Doktor. If you continue to act now, it will mean certain arrest and inevitably you'll be unable to help others in the future.'

Kersten agreed and resolved to return to his practice, but only a few days later he was involved in the most dangerous adventure of his entire rescue mission . . .

He was tucking into a crowded plate of chocolate cakes in the canteen at Prinz Albrechtstrasse at noon on 1 March 1941 when his two arch enemies, Heydrich and Rauter, entered and sat at a table near his. Neither of them spotted Kersten sitting only a few feet away. They were soon lost in conversation and oblivious to all around them. They must have imagined that there could be few more secure places to talk than in the canteen of the SS Headquarters – but they were wrong. Kersten strained his ears to catch a few of the words. The hush of the others in the canteen, silenced by Heydrich's presence, made it easier for him to hear the conversation.

Kersten's interest was especially keen for he knew that whatever they were to talk about would inevitably involve Holland which was Rauter's responsibility. He was the first to speak.

'The plan for the deportation of the Dutch to Poland is a masterpiece. The Reichsführer has excelled himself. It will rid the country of those we don't want. The Dutch have grown plump with inactivity.'

'They are swine of the lowest order,' Heydrich interjected. 'But soon that section of the problem will be dealt with. I've already got the outline plan from the Reichsführer's office and you should have your orders shortly.'

'Good, I shall make all the necessary preparations. With them gone we will have less trouble. The Dutch are becoming increasingly violent towards us and the SS in particular. My men have been stoned in the street, shot at and molested. The situation is intolerable but the Reichsführer has found the solution, and I'm all set to carry out his orders.'

Kersten had heard enough. The deportations of the past had been bad enough but now it was to be done on a massive scale. There was no doubt now that, careless of his own safety, he would have to act . . . and Himmler would be his target. He rose from his table and left without either of the two seeing him.

Kersten slept fitfully that night. He resolved to broach the subject of the Dutch deportation with Himmler the very next day.

Kersten arrived at Prinz Albrechtstrasse a little earlier than usual and made a point of going to see Brandt before taking the plunge with Himmler. Brandt was serious and preoccupied when Kersten entered his office. He had a folder in his hand and was studying it.

'Read that,' he said to Kersten.

The doctor took it. It was marked secret and contained details of the mass deportation of thousands of Dutch men, women, and children. Kersten told Brandt what he was going to do.

'But you are interfering with basic Nazi policy!' Brandt exploded. 'Himmler will never agree to change his plans. Look, Kersten, you have worked miracles up till now. I never dreamed that you would succeed as you have but what you suggest is impossible. He won't give in to you this time.'

'But he must!' Kersten demanded. 'According to this document he means to deport more than three million people to Lublin. He's going to march all the men right across Holland, Germany, and into Poland while the women and children go by ship and train. There's never been anything like it in the history of mankind. It's barbaric. He's got to be stopped! If I can't do it then somebody else must, but I've got to try no matter what.'

Kersten left a worried Brandt and made his way to Himmler's office where the Reichsführer was waiting for him. Himmler lay down on the long couch and undid his tunic and shirt, exposing his flabby torso. Kersten thrust his hands at the nerve centre and Himmler winced as the pain swept his body. Then the doctor began the massage, lulling his patient into tranquillity. If there was a right time to act, it was now.

'I hear that you mean to deport the majority of the Dutch to Poland,' Kersten stated in a composed, matter-of-fact tone. Himmler, instantly oblivious to his pain, sat bolt upright.

'What? Where did you hear that?' he demanded. 'That is a state secret!'

'I heard it in the most unlikely place – the SS staff canteen. Heydrich and Rauter were discussing it and I happened to be at the next table. I could not help but overhear their conversation.'

Himmler was thunderstruck.

'The fools! They might just as well have broadcast it!'

Now was the telling time for Kersten. Would Himmler trust him or had the time come for him to be 'silenced'?

'Herr Doktor,' Himmler began, 'I have to trust you. You have been taken into my confidence in the past and I have no reason to doubt your loyalty. Now I must place you once more on trust. I rely upon you to keep this to yourself. No one must know of this – no one.'

Kersten assured him that he would tell no one and continued his treatment. He had overcome one hurdle but there was another to be surmounted. He chose his moment with perfection and boldly came out with the first criticism he had dared level against Himmler to his face. As he kneaded the flesh, he remarked with genuine sincerity . . .

'You know, Herr Reichsführer, deporting the Dutch is a grave mistake. One that could well mark a black spot in your career.'

Kersten expected him to explode, but instead the Reichsführer smiled and looked up at his doctor.

'Kersten, my dear friend, as a doctor you are without peer but you are an innocent where politics are concerned.'

Himmler raised himself on one elbow and launched himself into his favourite topic.

'The exodus of the Dutch people is the brain-child of the Führer himself. It is a scheme of absolute brilliance. You must understand, Kersten, the problems we have in Poland. We conquered the country but the victory was not complete. You see, we have failed to win over the hearts of the people – they hate us. So, the Führer in his wisdom has decided to inject some Germanic blood into the country. The Dutch have that Germanic blood and in time, with the mixture of the two races, the minds of the Polish people will turn towards Germany, their rightful leaders. In the initial stages of the resettlement, the Poles will naturally revolt against the Dutch and the Dutch will have to turn to us for protection. In this way we will win over the Dutch as well. We will in effect have a greater Germany. Holland itself will be given over to the lower orders in our own society, the workers on the land. Brilliant, is it not?'

Kersten did not answer directly.

'Herr Reichsführer, you are right in your assumption that I am not aware of the political implications. I do not pretend to be knowledgeable on the subject but as your medical adviser I must express my grave concern about your health.'

Himmler's brow creased. Kersten had touched a nerve.

'My health?' he said quizzically.

'Yes, Herr Reichsführer. You are under considerable strain. Not long ago you told me that you had had orders to bring the SS up to a strength of one million in a matter of only two or three months. This means that you have to raise a virtual army in addition to your normal duties. No man can withstand such pressure and you are saying that above all this you are to organise the deportation of the Dutch to Poland. I can only say as a doctor that you will never survive such an undertaking.'

Himmler rose from the couch and paced the floor.

'I appreciate your concern, Kersten, but you must understand that I have no alternative. It is an order direct from the Führer.'

Kersten thought for a moment, wrestling in his mind for a way of breaking through Himmler's barrier of veneration for the Führer.

'I can see why the Führer has chosen such a dedicated man as yourself but surely he must realise that this added responsibility is beyond even you. If you take this on then one of the two major tasks, the increased strength of the SS and the deportation of the Dutch, must suffer. You cannot do both and the SS project must be the more important.'

'It's true that building up the SS is crucial but there's no way I can lessen my burden.'

'Yes, Herr Reichsführer, there is. You must postpone the deportation of the Dutch; put it off until the situation is eased, until victory has been won, then you can concentrate on it.'

'That's out of the question. The Führer has given explicit instructions that it's to be carried out without delay. Indeed I plan to begin the deportation on April the twentieth, the Führer's birthday. It will be a personal gift from me to him.'

'Then I must tell you that I shall not be able to sustain you in health through such a period of strain. I beg you, for your own sake, postpone the deportation.'

'Out of the question,' Himmler repeated resolutely.

In the weeks that followed, Kersten met the same stubborn refusal to give way. Nothing would sway Himmler and with each day the deportation drew closer.

Towards the end of March a strange occurrence took place which was to have a marked effect upon both men. Kersten's mental anguish about the fate of the Dutch caused him sleepless nights and he was working so hard treating Himmler that he now had almost no time for his other patients. And then it happened. First in one session and then in another Kersten's massage failed to relieve the Reichsführer's pain. He simply could not get the magic in his hands to work. Himmler was tortured by pain, while Kersten became a shadow of his former self. The destiny of a whole nation seemed to rest upon his shoulders. It was an awesome responsibility for him to carry. He had to admit to Himmler that he had lost his healing touch.

'It is hopeless, Herr Reichsführer. I told you that if you persisted with the amount of work you have taken on, you would be beyond my help. My hands are powerless to help you. As your doctor, I must insist that you set aside one of your tasks.'

Through his blinding pain, Himmler summoned the energy to rise to anger.

'Kersten! You must not persist with this attitude. It is impossible for me to postpone any of my work. As a doctor you must continue to try to relieve my pain. It is your duty. Now continue at once.'

Kersten tried, but failed. He returned to Himmler's office to give him treatment as many as ten times in a single day but he made no impression. Himmler was ghost-like in appearance, drawn and gaunt from constant pain and as the days passed his condition got progressively worse.

The crunch came in the opening days of April 1941. Germany invaded Yugoslavia and Himmler felt it necessary to be there at that country's demise. He ordered Kersten to accompany him so that he might continue his treatment. Throughout the campaign, Himmler was confined to his bed where Kersten was with him day and night. The only time he rose was when ordered to attend a meeting with Hitler. At every session of treatment, Kersten repeated his warning. Finally in despair the truth began to dawn and one morning, twisted in pain, he admitted to Kersten that he was right and that the deportation would have to be postponed. The tears were in his eyes as he told his doctor.

'I have failed, Kersten. I have failed my Führer.'

'No, Herr Reichsführer, you have not failed. You are simply being sensible. The Führer would not demand the impossible of you.'

'Yes, but what am I to say to him? I gave my word as a loyal German that I would fulfil my promise with regard to the Dutch question but now I cannot do it. My body simply will not stand up to my demands upon it.'

Kersten assumed the role of confidant once more, adopting an almost paternal attitude towards the pathetic creature prostrate in his bed.

'You will tell the Führer that the time is not right; that, because of conditions at sea – the lack of ships and the threat of the Allied navy – and the congested roads between Holland and Germany, the project must be postponed.'

'Yes,' Himmler said dejectedly, 'that is what I must do. But I must have the physical strength to resume my duties otherwise I shall have failed my Führer completely.'

'I am confident that when you have informed the Führer of your decision, I shall be able to help you once more.'

Now that he had Himmler's assurance and was relieved of anxiety Kersten found almost immediately that his hands obeyed his wishes. Gradually he was able to relieve the Reichsführer of some of his pain. Himmler admitted that it was nothing short of a miracle. But then came a setback.

During one of the sessions the telephone rang. It was 'good news'. Yugoslavia had fallen. At once Himmler was a new man; buoyant, jovial and triumphant. But it concerned Kersten for, revitalised by the news from the Yugoslav front, Himmler might change his mind about the deportation of the Dutch. The doctor held his breath.

'We triumph once more!' Himmler roared victoriously. 'Germany soars on the crest of a wave. Nothing stands in our way. I have been recalled to see the Führer in Berlin immediately!'

The fate of the Dutch was once more in the balance and Kersten was on tenterhooks. But good fortune was on his side. During the train journey to Berlin, Himmler suffered another attack – a fierce, crippling cramp. Kersten went to his aid but this time he prolonged the treatment, telling Himmler that he would have to take things easy for some time to come.

Himmler was obliged to agree and not long afterwards told Kersten that the resettlement of the Dutch had been postponed indefinitely. Hitler had approved it himself.

Himmler and Brandt left Berlin to attend a meeting in Munich and since Himmler was out of pain there was no need for Kersten to accompany him. It was then that Heydrich struck. Kersten was ordered to meet Heydrich at his office. He suspected that whatever the Gestapo boss had in store for him would not be good, so he took the precaution of calling in at Himmler's office and instructing one of his staff to contact the Reichsführer immediately and inform him that he had been summoned by Heydrich.

With that done he went on to keep the appointment. Heydrich was waiting for him. When the mock pleasantries had been completed, Heydrich engaged in some verbal prevarication before showing his hand.

'I must tell you, Kersten, that it is my firm belief that you played a major part in persuading the Reichsführer SS to postpone the resettlement of the Dutch.'

Kersten tried to fob off the whole suggestion.

'Oh come, come, I am a doctor, not a politician. How could I possibly have achieved what you say?'

'Of that I am not certain but I am confident that what I say is true and that you are a traitor to the Reich. It would not surprise me if you are an agent of the Allies. You were a close friend of the Dutch Royal family and I suspect your loyalties lie there. Furthermore you manoeuvred your way into the friendship of the Reichsführer SS to gain his trust and influence over him.'

'That is simply not so,' Kersten insisted. 'It was the Reichsführer himself who called upon me!'

Heydrich would hear none of it.

'Kersten, you are a threat to the Reich and because of that I am placing you under arrest.'

Kersten knew that argument was hopeless. Heydrich was quite capable of arranging his exposure before Himmler returned and, with the deed done, the Reichsführer would be in no position to come to his aid. But just as Kersten was resigning himself to his fate, the telephone rang in an outer office. Heydrich went to answer it and returned a minute later, looking decidedly sheepish. He sat down at his desk and forced a smile, then continued talking but without mentioning the telephone call.

'You seem extraordinarily well informed about the business of the SS, Kersten. I am interested to know exactly where you get your information. One day, Herr Doktor, I shall find out and then your friend the Reichsführer will not be so ready to come to your aid.'

'I don't understand,' Kersten said innocently.

'You understand all right, Kersten. That telephone call was from the Reichsführer. I have been ordered to release you at once.'

His eyes narrowed maliciously. He had been foiled in his attempt to discredit Kersten and this heightened his resolve to crush him. But he was destined never to have that satisfaction. Later that year Heydrich was assassinated in Czechoslovakia. However, his removal only made way for someone equally brutal, Ernst Kaltenbrunner. Meanwhile Himmler's condition got progressively worse as the months passed.

Towards the end of 1942 he was unusually preoccupied. Germany had suffered a series of reverses and there was a general air of gloom at SS Headquarters. Himmler was edgy, but the cause of his nervousness was not simply the military situation. At last he turned to Kersten for advice.

'Herr Doktor, you have been a good friend over the years and I am in your debt, but now I must trust you with knowledge so secret that if it were revealed to any but a few people, it might bring down the Third Reich.'

Himmler thought for a moment, paused in consideration, wondering whether or not he should take this momentous step. Then suddenly he braced himself with determination. The decision was made.

'But first,' he began, 'I must ask you a question. Your skill is great. I have seen that. But I do not know how far it extends. For instance, could you treat someone who could not sleep and suffered from severe migraine and dizzy spells?'

'I might. But it would depend entirely upon what was causing these symptoms. Obviously I would have to examine the patient to determine the cause. Who . . .?'

Himmler interrupted. He looked more agitated than ever. He was flustered and his hands trembled.

'What I am about to tell you must be repeated to no one. Is that clearly understood? No one.'

'Herr Reichsführer, you can be assured of my absolute discretion.'

But even then, Himmler seemed too frightened to reveal his secret. Instead, as if feeling that it would in some way lessen his guilt, Himmler thrust a bulky file into Kersten's hands.

'Here,' he said. 'It is all in there. Read it.'

The cover of the file carried the caution that its contents were top secret. Kersten opened it and his eyes stared in disbelief. The title alone showed clearly why Himmler had been so reluctant. The file was a complete account of the illness suffered by Adolf Hitler.

Kersten sat down and read through the twenty-odd pages of text. They went into the greatest detail, clearly holding nothing back. As a young man, Hitler had contracted syphilis. He had been treated in hospital and had come out 'cured' but, in 1937, the syphilis had returned, and was more virulent than ever. As time passed signs of paralysis became evident, his hands trembled and he found deep sleep impossible, even after taking drugs. The headaches became fierce and his mind was in a constant torment. As he read through the detailed documents, Kersten could not help but reflect upon how these symptoms might have contributed to Hitler's irrational behaviour.

He finished reading through the file and realised the enormity of Himmler's dilemma. If such information were to become generally known, the effect could mean the downfall of Hitler and possibly the Nazis with him. If the Allies got to know of it, the propaganda they could obtain from it would be immeasurably greater than anything they had so far succeeded in amassing from within the Reich.

Kersten handed the file back to Himmler.

'I'm afraid that there is nothing I can do. The illness has progressed too far for me to be of any help to him. As far as I know, there is no cure for it. It can only get progressively worse and his condition will deteriorate until eventually he will die.'

'That cannot be allowed to happen!' Himmler blurted out desperately. 'The Führer is too precious to humanity to be allowed to die, at least until his mission in life is fulfilled. Above all his image must be preserved as an example to those who come after him. He has a personal physician who gives him daily injections of some concoction which he claims will prevent the disease from getting worse.'

'I'm afraid you cannot hold out any hope of that helping him. As I say, so far medical science has failed to find anything that will arrest his condition. You must face it, Herr Reichsführer, Hitler is doomed.'

'That is what I feared you would say. What am I to do?'

Himmler was baffled, bewildered, and unable to think clearly. He worshipped Hitler and yet Hitler was no longer capable of conducting his own affairs, let alone those of Germany. Himmler was beside himself with anxiety and Kersten left him pacing the floor, troubled far beyond Kersten's help.

When he left the office he went straight to Brandt. He had to confide in someone, share the secret. When he told him what had just happened, Brandt almost fainted with shock.

'Never mention this again to Himmler, otherwise he might realise what he has said and have you removed.'

'I understand only too well, Brandt. And I know there is nothing I can do. You know, the future of the Reich lies to a very large extent in Himmler's own hands. Can he leave Hitler to direct operations, the prosecution of the war, a man whom syphilis has made incapable of rational thought? If Himmler loves Germany as he claims he does then he must get rid of Hitler. The man is already mad and can only get worse.'

Kersten left it at that, and for the following week saw Himmler every day without mentioning the subject of Hitler's health. Neither did Himmler mention it, which gave Kersten to believe that he must have found some solution.

During one of the sessions of treatment, Himmler asked Kersten outright if he had thought of a way of treating the Führer. Kersten said he had not, but that he had given it considerable thought. He reiterated what he had already made clear – that complete madness would follow.

'The future of Germany is at stake, my friend,' Himmler said in despair. 'Without Hitler the Reich will collapse, of that I am sure. Especially now, when we are on the very brink of total victory.'

'I have said to you before, Herr Reichsführer, that I am no politician, but it is clear to me that only a man who has clarity of mind can rule a nation. The Führer does not have that. The consequences of his remaining in power could have a profound effect upon the future of Germany and the occupied territories. He is no longer the man he was when he came to power. With this illness he is incapable of steering a true course for Germany. Hitler has no right to be the Führer.'

Kersten realised that these were dangerous words but he had caught the mood of the conversation and guessed that Himmler was thinking along similar lines.

'You are right. It's a terrible thing to admit, yet one must face facts. But you see my dilemma. As a soldier I am sworn in allegiance to Adolf Hitler. When I and my SS took that oath along with the entire Wehrmacht, it was an oath before God to follow and obey Hitler. How can I now even consider doing anything that might bring him down? If I did, I would be seen as power-hungry, seeking to become Führer myself. It is unthinkable.'

'Then you are prepared to see Germany crumble once more, the way she did in 1918? For that's what will happen if Hitler is allowed to remain in power!'

'I know! I know! I know!' Himmler was close to tears and he buried his head in his hands. 'I can't do it – I can't.' He looked up at Kersten. 'There is still time. Hitler has not reached the point when he cannot control himself. Something will come up to save him. It must!' But Hitler was long past the point of no return. Kersten knew it, and left Himmler to his misery. The subject was never brought up again.

Throughout the year that followed, Kersten succeeded in obtaining the release of small numbers of people who had been arrested by the Gestapo, and in the process further alienated Kaltenbrunner. The risk had to be taken, despite warnings from friends that he was a prime target for assassination by the Gestapo. Undeterred, he continued badgering Himmler to release more. By now the death camps had reached a murderous state of perfection. Kersten, knowing this, sought to find a way of rescuing more souls from the gas chamber.

He found himself in an unusual and awkward position when Finland entered the war as an ally of Germany. As an officer in the Finnish Reserve Army, he was then indirectly a supporter of the very regime he hated. He was even more hemmed in than before, now that he had no free country, but he was duty bound to be loyal to Finland.

In September 1943, he was summoned to Finland so that he could put the Finnish government in the picture about what he had learned from Himmler. But Himmler was jealous of any contacts Kersten had outside Germany and when the doctor asked for permission to leave the country and return to Finland for a short stay, Himmler became anxious. Kersten explained that it was a matter of courtesy. He was under an obligation to return because he was an officer in the reserve army. The Reichsführer very reluctantly agreed but ordered him to find out why the Finnish government had not yet handed over the Jews who were living in their country.

The problem was further aggravated when the Swedish Ambassador in Berlin called on Kersten as he was preparing to leave for Finland. The Ambassador asked him if he would visit the Swedish capital en route to Finland and discuss with government officials something of the utmost importance. He could at that time be no more explicit than that. Kersten agreed, but there was an obstacle in his path – Himmler. How could he explain the visit without arousing suspicion? After much thought, he succeeded by telling Himmler that there were Finnish soldiers in hospital in Stockholm who were in need of his treatment. Himmler gave his consent and Kersten left Germany.

Kersten felt the flush of freedom when he arrived in Stockholm. There he could breathe again, away from the suppression and suspicion that reigned in Germany, away from the constant threat of the Gestapo, away from the war. But even there, he could not escape it for long. He met representatives of the Swedish government who pointed out that their country was under severe pressure from the Allies to enter the war on their side. Sweden had declined but had promised to do all she could to help the Jews who were being persecuted in Germany. The Swedish Minister of Foreign Affairs asked Kersten if he could bring his influence to bear on Himmler. After a plan had been outlined, he agreed to try. It called for him to persuade Himmler to release Jews from Germany and allow them to be resettled in Sweden. The whole operation was to be carried out with the help of the Red Cross under the direction of Count Folke Bernadotte. Discussions about the new humanitarian plan went on for several days before Kersten made his way to Finland and from there back to Germany.

He pondered how he could persuade Himmler to release the Jews. There was no doubt that to accomplish a task of this magnitude he would need allies; friends in high places who could help him. It was too much for one man to handle but he did know of two men who, over the years, had shown sympathy with his cause and both were in influential positions. They were General Gottlob Berger and Colonel Walter Schellenberg. The latter was a dynamic young SS officer who had won his spurs in Heydrich's intelligence service and had his sights set upon being the youngest General in the Wehrmacht. He had come into contact with Kersten when Himmler asked the doctor to examine him. There was nothing wrong with the young officer, but Himmler was conscious of his strong ambition and wanted Kersten to assess his character, using a routine examination as an excuse. During the examination, Schellenberg offered the hand of friendship and gave Kersten a promise that he would help him in any way he could. From then on, Schellenberg had proved a useful voice in securing the release of individual Jews.

Berger was the antithesis of the ambitious young colonel. A stickler for discipline and an army officer through and through, his thoughts were directed almost exclusively towards winning the war. As a commander of the *Waffen* SS, he was in a strong position. The *Waffen* SS was the fighting arm of the SS as distinct from the men who carried out the exterminations at the death camps. He was a soldier who found the slaughter of the Jews repugnant. Like Schellenberg, Kersten first met Berger when Himmler ordered him to have a medical examination. At first the General disliked Kersten, but as the treatment progressed they built up a bond of friendship which was to prove beneficial to both of them.

When Kersten tested these two men about the plan for the resettlement of the Jews in Sweden their reactions were more favourable than he dared hope. Both promised him their support.

Kersten felt reassured. Over the months of treatment

that followed he continually brought up the subject of the concentration camps and in particular the incarceration of the Dutch, Norwegian and Danish Jews. As time went by and the course of the war took turn after turn for the worse for Germany, Himmler's fanatical loyalty to the Führer showed signs of crumbling. The time now seemed right for Kersten to put his proposal to Himmler.

However, on 20 July 1944, Colonel Claus von Stauffenberg planted a bomb under the table at Hitler's headquarters in Prussia, in an attempt to kill him. It was unsuccessful, but the shock and Hitler's miraculous escape reaffirmed Himmler's blind faith in the Führer. Hitler demanded revenge upon the army, whom he blamed for the attempt on his life and ordered the execution of thousands of people, most of whom had had nothing to do with it. Himmler and Kaltenbrunner were appointed executioners.

Himmler went about the witch-hunt with customary diligence and the strain brought on a serious recurrence of his illness. Kersten was directed to accompany him on his train in East Prussia. He quickly packed his things and was about to leave when a despatch rider arrived with an urgent note from Schellenberg. It warned Kersten that Kaltenbrunner had set an ambush for him at a point on his usual route through Oranienburg. He was to be killed, irrespective of the consequences.

Kersten was stunned by the note but it was not entirely unexpected. He decided to take an alternative route and in due course arrived safely at Himmler's train. He lost no time in showing the Reichsführer the warning note. Himmler could not believe that a subordinate of his would dare to plan such a thing. Schellenberg could, he reasoned, have been mistaken or for some personal reason have been bent upon discrediting Kaltenbrunner. So Himmler set about checking the story with reliable sources within the Kaltenbrunner organisation. A plot had indeed been laid to kill Kersten. Himmler was furious, but Kaltenbrunner was a valued member of his organisation and he could ill afford to dispense with him. He therefore planned to chastise him for the misdemeanour by embarrassing him and ordered him to have lunch with himself and Kersten that very day.

There was an uneasy tension around the lunch table when the three of them got together. Kaltenbrunner by his very attitude left Kersten and Himmler in no doubt about his hatred of the doctor. Himmler made no reference to the attempted assassination but emphasised that if Kersten were to be murdered, his murderer would quickly follow him to the grave.

'Let me make it clear,' Himmler began, fixing Kaltenbrunner with a menacing gaze, 'if anything should happen to Dr Kersten, I shall hold you personally responsible and you will pay the penalty. Do you understand, Kaltenbrunner?'

Kaltenbrunner nodded. He had lost.

Kersten felt the time was again ripe to approach Himmler with his proposals but he again had to stay his hand, as events changed the Reichsführer's mood daily. Months passed and then, by a curious and ironic incident, Kersten's chance came.

Following the attempt on Hitler's life, none of the top brass in the army was safe and many perished in the purge. Civilians also suffered. One of them was Carl Wentzel, a friend of Kersten's. Wentzel was sentenced to death for his part in the bomb plot and although Kersten did not believe that he could get a pardon for him, he did try to get a reprieve – and Himmler granted it, giving his word of honour that Wentzel would not be hanged. Then on 8 December 1944, Kersten learned to his horror that his friend had been executed. In a towering rage he confronted Himmler.

'You have gone back on your word as an officer!

You, the Reichsführer, who places so much on your word. It is worthless!'

Himmler sat open-mouthed and hurt at the accusation. He attempted to plead with Kersten and explain, but the doctor turned on his heel and slammed the door in Himmler's face.

In the outer office, he almost collided with Brandt. Still in a rage he told him what had happened and Brandt tried to explain that the matter had been out of Himmler's hands. The secretary eventually succeeded in pacifying Kersten. It was true that Himmler had had no say in the matter but the doctor was determined to make the Reichsführer atone for letting him down. He returned to Himmler's office.

'Brandt has explained to me that there was nothing you could have done. But it does not detract from the fact that you made a promise and you failed to keep it. You broke your word!'

Himmler pleaded with him: 'I shall make retribution, of that you can be sure. Just simply ask and you shall see that I am a man of my word.'

Kersten knew that this was the time to strike and he made his demands. Himmler, anxious to make amends, agreed to them, in part at least.

Kersten's achievements were staggering. Himmler agreed to release one hundred Norwegian and Danish prisoners right away, as well as some 3000 Polish, French, Belgian and Dutch women as soon as the Swedes were ready to take them. In addition, all Scandinavian prisoners would be moved to camps outside the range of Allied bombers where they would be safe from accidental attack. But Kersten wanted more. He knew that Sweden could take 20,000 Jews and he urged Himmler to release them. However, that was outside the Reichsführer's power. Hitler would be certain to find out about it. Instead, he promised to have between two and three thousand released whenever the opportunity arose. The chance came two months later when 2700 Jews were ready to be sent by train to the death camps. Instead, on Himmler's orders, they were diverted to the Swiss border where they were handed over to the Swiss authorities.

The Allies were by then closing in on every side and defeat was only a short time away. Hitler ordered all the concentration camps to be blown up as the Allies approached. Not a single Jew was to survive. Kersten heard of this maniacal directive from the Swedish government who asked him to do what he could to stop it. He challenged Himmler.

'Yes, it is true,' he admitted. 'It is the Führer's wish.'

'His wish? The wish of a madman? Hitler no longer thinks like a sane person. He hasn't for a long time. And you are going to obey him?'

'I must. Those are my orders,' Himmler explained, as if that was all that had to be said.

'You can't do it. There are 800,000 people in the camps and you are going to wipe them out at a stroke? In the name of humanity, you must not.'

Kersten tried to put forward a reasoned argument.

'Herr Reichsführer, you are without doubt the most powerful man in Germany now. The German army is at the point of total collapse. You have the SS at your disposal ... You cannot allow Hitler to dishonour Germany in the moment of defeat. You must extricate her by showing mercy.' He paused. 'History will remember you as a man of mercy,' he lied.

Himmler simply said there was nothing he could do. But Kersten was not prepared to leave it at that. He argued no further with Himmler that day but told Schellenberg and Berger, who in turn approached Himmler with the same argument. At last, Himmler relented and signed a document directing that the camps were not to be blown up, no more Jews were to be executed, and Sweden would be allowed to send food parcels to the Jewish prisoners. Furthermore, and perhaps most surprising of all, he agreed to meet a representative of the World Jewish Congress with a view to releasing 5000 Jews.

Norbert Masur was chosen as the representative to meet Himmler, and Kersten arranged to escort him from Stockholm to Germany. They flew in a specially provided Luftwaffe aircraft and as they approached Berlin they could clearly hear the roar of the Russian guns far below on the outskirts of the great city. It was 19 April and the war was almost over. But there were still fanatics like Hitler who would bring the world down with them. One of them was Martin Bormann, the head of the Nazi Party, who was doing all he could to reinstate the decision to blow up the concentration camps. Schellenberg warned Kersten when he arrived in Berlin that he thought Himmler would succumb to Bormann's persuasion. It was a final race against time.

The fateful meeting was to take place at Kersten's estate and it was the small hours of the morning when Himmler finally arrived, resplendent in his best SS uniform, to meet the representative of the race he had set about wiping out.

Himmler was surprisingly unperturbed by the whole affair and conducted himself in a reasonably civilised manner towards the Jew. But he did devote most of the dialogue to the shortcomings of the Semites, getting in what he must have realised would be a final jab at the Jews.

At dawn Himmler finally agreed to guarantee the lives of all the remaining Jews. Everyone at that meeting was exhausted. Kersten and the others had accomplished the impossible.

With the meeting over, Kersten led Himmler out to his waiting car. The morning was bleak and overcast. Himmler, perhaps sensing that the end was near, shook Kersten by the hand. There were tears streaming down his face. Himmler, Reichsführer SS, butcher of millions, was steeped in self-pity. He was doomed. The car roared off down the drive. Kersten watched it go with its pathetic passenger. They would never meet again.

Himmler disappeared, seeking in vain to gain a refuge from those who were hunting him down. The war in Europe ended with Himmler still on the run, but on 21 May 1945 he was caught by British guards in North West Germany. He committed suicide in his cell before he could be brought to trial.

Brandt's willingness to help Kersten in these desperate times during the war counted for nothing. He had drafted the directives which had sent millions to the gas chambers and they carried his damning signature. He was hanged.

General Berger was sentenced to twenty-five years in prison for war-crimes but was released after serving only five. Kersten's other major aide, Schellenberg, was sentenced to six years, but was released after two. He died within a short time of his release.

Kersten went to Sweden after the war and set up practice there with Swedish citizenship, but his troubles were not over. There were still those who suspected him of having been a willing collaborator with Himmler. He had treated some of the highest-ranking Nazis and as such was suspect. When this cloud of suspicion became known to many of those whose lives had been saved as a result of his courage, they demanded an enquiry. It was one of the most searching and detailed of the post-mortems of the war, and the full extent of Kersten's courage was revealed. As a result he was honoured and decorated by the Dutch government and praised by the thousands he had rescued from execution. He died in April 1960.

Bibliography

Baker, Alan, *Merrill's Marauders* (Pan/Ballantine, 1972)
Barker, Ralph, *Down in the Drink* (Chatto & Windus, 1955)
Delarue, Jacques, *The History of the Gestapo* (Macdonald, 1964)
Halstead, Ivor, *Heroes of the Atlantic* (The Right Book Club, 1941)
Hart, Sir Basil Liddell, *History of the Second World War* (Cassell, 1970)
Hastings, Macdonald, *More Men of Glory* (Hulton, 1959)
History of the Second World War (Purnell)
Kessel, Joseph, *The Magic Touch* (Hart-Davis, 1961)
Lyall, Gavin, *Freedom's Battle: The War in the Air* (Hutchinson, 1968)
MacIntyre, Donald, *Narvik* (Evans Brothers, 1959)
Manvell, Roger and Fraenkel, Heinrich, *Heinrich Himmler* (Heinemann, 1965)
Padfield, Peter, *The Battleship Era* (Hart-Davis, 1972)
Secrets and Stories of the War: vols. 1 and 2 (Reader's Digest, 1963)
Stubbs, Bernard, *The Navy at War* (Faber, 1940)
Taylor, John W. R., *Aircraft of World War II* (Odhams, 1965)
Vian, Sir Phillip, *Action This Day* (Muller)
Whiting, Charles, *The Battle for Twelveland* (Leo Cooper, 1975)
Wighton, Charles, *Eichmann: His Career and Crimes* (Odhams, 1961)

Winton, John, *Freedom's Battle: The War at Sea* (Hutchinson, 1967)
Young, Peter, *A Short History of the Second World War* (Arthur Barker, 1966)